DOUBLE JOYE

Two Short Stories by

Stanley B. Joye

This book is a work of fiction. Places, events, and situations in this story are purely fictional. Any resemblance to actual persons, living or dead, is coincidental.

ISBN: 1-4140-1375-2 (e-book)
ISBN: 1-4140-1376-0 (Paperback)

Library of Congress Control Number: 2003097834

This book is printed on acid free paper.

Printed in the United States of America
Bloomington, IN

1stBooks — rev. 11/10/03

RECOVER THE TOMB

ONE

Jerson is riding wildly across the valley, if only he can get to the mountain pass in time. The dust is leaving a wake behind him in the hot desert air. He almost loses his breath as he swats at the horse to ride faster. Sweat is pouring off his forehead into his eyes and burning. He keeps trying to wipe it off but can't waste a step of the horse's gait; he must keep in rhythm. His mind races from the recent events and the images of the large iron men loom larger in his memory distorted by fear. The invincible breastplate with the large red cross on it seems ever present. What did he do? Why are they chasing me he wonders? He doesn't have to wonder about their intent though; their drawn swords being swung through the air give a clear meaning. He can still hear the thunderous hoofs of the horses behind him. He didn't get a chance to see how many, but what does it matter, one is too many! They've got to be as hot as he is and tiring, maybe hotter because of the armor they're wearing. They've got to be just men like him even though they seem like demons. They're cruel and

3

murderous and somehow feel righteous in their deeds. The pass is just up ahead and if he makes it he can lose them in the many winding trails that branch off this way and that many times. He takes the first trail to the left; they follow not too far behind. The next trail is a fork, he goes right, but they can see the dust kicked up from the horse's hoofs and follow to the right. The trail riding is slowing them down; they don't know the terrain. Jerson gallops full speed ahead going up a steep incline, he knows the path goes along the top both ways then dips down into a chasm. His pursuers follow but are slowed by the incline and hesitate at the top, their own dust catching up to them. They can't see clearly for a minute because of it, and when it clears, there's no sign of Jerson!

Jerson jumps off his horse to walk him into a caved area he knows here in this chasm. Also there's water in a small spring hole. He's so thirsty that his mouth and lips are sticking together. He drinks slowly and long at the cool water in the hole then gives way for the horse to drink. He's caught his breath back by now and goes into one of the caves with the horse, here he shouldn't be found. Now he can sleep and regain his strength for tomorrow's ride.

It's morning and the sunlight streams down through the craggy cliffs around the chasm, Jerson is up and stirring. He drinks some water then leads his horse over to drink. 'Drink fully boy, we have to ride across the rest of the desert today' he says. As the horse drinks, he walks up the trail a little to look out and see if anyone is there. It's quiet all around and no one is close. He mounts his horse and slowly rides out back onto the desert valley floor looking around as he goes. He sees no one or anything, just the desolate arid landscape and the shadows made by the sun.

Justin, the commander who dispatched the men who chased Jerson is looking out over the desert also, but from the other end miles away. The men had returned with the report they had lost the man they were chasing in a chasm and they would have been lost themselves if they pursued any farther. Well, just another lone heathen probably not much value to his cause he thinks. What an awful place this is he goes on, desolate and barren, extremes in weather, dusty and windy and nothing like the green hills of home. All this way he had come on this noblest of quests, to recover the tomb of the Savior from the heathen. This is near the land of the Covenants and the Ishmaels, historically brothers but always fighting each other. Time to move on to the City of Peace and join the others. He secretly wishes he had been here in the early days to take part in the victory over the Ismaels holding the city, which would have been glorious. This was a futile excursion into this hellish landscape and they hadn't found any Mongs out here. The Mongs had conquered Persia and soon would be moving westward. These are the same vicious fighters from the far east land of the famed conqueror Ghengis, only now their offspring follow his offspring, a conqueror just as fearsome; Kublai!

Jerson finally comes to the small town he had left earlier coincidentally on the same mission as Justin, to look for Mong invaders coming across the desert. He rides into the camp of the nomads.

'Jerson, you've finally returned. What news of the invaders?' Asks Abul, the nomad's leader.

'I didn't see any Mongs out there, they must still be in Persia. I ran into some Crucifers though and they chased me for awhile but I lost them.'

'What irony... the City of Peace... in war, time and time again. The Ishmaels fight the Covenants while both are under siege from the Crucifers... and now a threat from the Mongs for us all. There are too many enemies here!'

'Jerson, that's a strange name...' says a young man in the group.

'Really? Well what's your name?'

'Albert'

'Albert, now that's strange... and you have pale skin, strange also...'

'I was one of the Crucifers but managed to escape from them and go out on my own.'

'Really? Are you part of us nomads now?'

'Yes, I find this a much better life for me' answers Albert.

'Well, my family has been in this group for generations' states Jerson 'and my name comes from one of them back at the time of the first Mong conquests during the days of the legendary city of Dorian.'

'That's fascinating, I've heard some about that legend since I've been out here.'

'How do we know you're not a spy from the Crucifers?'

Suddenly Abul interrupts, 'Jerson, Jerson… You know we wouldn't take in just anyone knowing nothing about them. Albert was found wandering around the city alone, often chased by Crucifers trying to kill him. We heard from people we know that he indeed was a deserter and his life was in danger. We asked him to join us and take on our dress and mannerisms so he may be safe from the Crucifers. So far they haven't found him out and probably will not.'

'So Albert, why don't you come to my tent for the evening meal and we can get acquainted?'

'I'd be honored Jerson, it seems you hold great respect among these people.'

In about an hour it is time for the evening meal. Most of the nomads have a small fire outside their own tents to cook on; occasionally they all get together for a feast on certain holidays. Jerson has his fire going well and brings out a hindquarter of a freshly slaughtered lamb. He skewers it with a large sharp tipped stick and places it on two supporting sticks to roast. The air smells of roasting meats and spices everywhere. Soon Albert shows up at Jerson's tent.

'Hello again Jerson'

7

'Albert, glad you made it. I'm roasting some lamb, we can eat soon.'

'I've brought some ale to drink that I was able to get from the Crucifers, have you ever had it?'

'Can't say that I have…what is it?'

'It's a fermented drink we have back in Europe. But I think it actually started in Egypt.'

'Oh yeah, I've heard of it. But I've always been a wine drinker. I'd still like to try some.'

'Of course, where's your goblet?'

'Inside… make yourself at home.'

So Albert finds a few goblets and takes two and pours some ale and brings them outside where Jerson is.

'Here we go. Let's have a toast… to this nomad life and good friendship, especially new ones as ours, and to long life.'

They toast and drink heartily.

'I kind of like this stuff, but it's a little bitter.'

'Well you'll either learn to like the bitterness or ignore it. The more drunk you get the more you don't notice it!'

Jerson belches right away and laughs.

'Oh yeah, you'll do that often with this ale… and piss a lot too!' says Albert.

'Really? Well I don't see that as a good effect of this drink.'

'Sure it's good, cleans you out inside!'

'Well this lamb is looking good, a little more and we can dig in…'

After the two feast on the lamb awhile, they settle back on a carpet and with a slight buzz on start to philosophize.

'So Albert, what are the Crucifers all about?'

'Religious and political fanatics I think. They preach that they are on a godly crusade to recover the tomb of the Savior from the Ishmaels who had control over the City of Peace. And they've done it too, for now.'

'Now this is supposed to be the same Savior of the Loways?' asks Jerson.

'Yeah, kind of I think, from what little I know of the Loways.'

'Well I was brought up under Loway teachings from my family, some past relatives lived with them for awhile. They're a very peaceful lot; they believe the way of salvation is not proud and forceful but meek and humble and lowly. That's where they get their name from, and they're not warlike at all.'

'Yeah we have that teaching in our Book also, but no one seems to take it seriously, they focus on judging and condemning everybody, especially anyone who doesn't believe exactly the way they do. They also covet political power and iron rule of the people' Albert continues, 'and that's why I've deserted. I no longer can stand the hypocrisy and cruelty of my kind. My arrogance and idealism from my younger days has diminished with an awareness of other ways... and I'm growing older. I see this evil in all kinds of people, but I also see those with love too, genuine love of life and others and God. I wish to be with more of these people.'

'You mean you don't have any of those kind?' questions Jerson.

'I suppose, I just didn't look for them, I was focused on the strong and dominating.'

'Yeah, but the problem is that the powerful tread on the meek and often destroy them. That's why we keep on moving.'

'Well I no longer have a choice but to keep on moving, they kill deserters if they catch them.'

'Don't be caught! It's easy to disappear out here, and don't ever go back around them even if you're tempted.'

Albert laughs a little and says 'Tempted? I will hardly be tempted to return to those bastards…'

'So what did you learn of the Savior from them?' asks Jerson.

'I didn't listen much… a lot about keeping commandments and not doing bad things and thinking bad thoughts or else you need to suffer now… or when you die you go to hell to burn!'

Jerson starts laughing 'ha ha ha! No wonder the Crucifers are the cruel sons of bitches they are, no one can do that all the time! So they try to force others and themselves to be holy, only making themselves blinded failing hypocrites and the whole damn thing as unholy as you can get!'

'Well, the Ishmaels and Covenants aren't much better!' replies Albert.

'And all the filthy dogs are here together, how convenient! Maybe they'll eliminate each other completely and we can live in peace for a change!'

'Yeah, that would be poetic justice but not about to happen I'm afraid. How do you feel about the Savior Jerson?'

'The Savior is more like a friend to me than a savior, although I embrace his salvation. Since I was a kid his spirit comes to visit me sometimes. I know it when the earth seems at peace and I feel at peace too. The world and all the worries slip away. I can only bask in this place like you would in the sunshine and it seems I can remember every other time I was like this. But I feel this deep longing and I sense eternity and maybe even heaven, and that's his kingdom… heaven. I feel like I can almost talk to him and reach out and touch him. And sometimes when I'm talking or sharing with others in the spirit of love whether believers or not, I can feel his spirit.'

'That's very nice' says Albert 'I think I've had that kind of thing happen to me for a fleeting moment or so here and there.'

So Jerson and Albert go on and on about their lives, their loves and adventures only interrupted by Jerson's and occasionally Albert's constant bladder relief. When it's very late they hug heartily like brothers do and return to their tents for sleep.

TWO

Justin has returned to the City of Peace with his men. He immediately meets with Martin, the man in charge, to report his findings.

'Justin my man, you've returned. What news from the desert?'

'We found no Mongs out there or anything appearing to be a gathering of them. They haven't left Persia yet is my guess, but you know they will sooner or later.'

'Is that area a good place for battle?'

'Not at all. It's hot, dry and hellish. There are too many places to hide in the surrounding mountains and gorges. There is no water there either' replies Justin.

'I think its too far north for the Mongs to attack. They want the shortest distance between themselves and the City of Peace. They'll probably go south then straight across west to us' says Martin.

'What if we take the fight to them?' asks Justin.

'Not a bad idea, certainly worth considering…'

'And I mean right into Persia… we drive them out and we're heroes to these people.'

'Yes that's good but not an easy task I'm afraid. Kublai is just as ruthless as Ghengis was, and Ghengis couldn't be stopped.'

'That was long ago, we've defeated all who have tried to stop us coming here, we can defeat this bloody Mong dog as well' states Justin proudly.

'Well the good thing is that we will not be the only enemy to the Mongs. All who live here are in danger of conquest. And all those to the west and south are in danger also. This means that however much they disdain us, we all have a common enemy and it would behoove them to take our side against the Mongs. So we may have some help here which we certainly can use.'

'Yes, that's probably true. But I wouldn't trust any of them for a moment, we must always watch our backs and when the Mongs are done we must reinstate our power among them' replies Justin.

'You mean another slaughter of Covenants and Ishmaels like in the beginning?' questions Martin.

'No, no of course not!' replies Justin 'just a show of power and a declaration of our authority here.'

'Very well, that's more like it. I have no stomach for slaughter except for the revenge I once suffered against the Ishmaels for slaughtering many Loways and Crucifers in the Holy city. I haven't told you, but recently we have received some word that the concerns over Kublai go as far as Egypt. They're actually preparing their troops today and inquiring about the possibility of a unified front of all this land to defeat the invaders. We've sent word of our intentions to engage Kublai and of our acceptance of unification for this cause.'

'I don't like it' replies Justin 'after we defeat Kublai they'll be prepared and ready to turn and fight us to expel us from this land, we're not exactly welcomed here!'

'I don't think so, we'll have a bond of victory over a common enemy and I think they will honor us for awhile before turning against us again.'

'Yes, I suppose you're right. But for now we ought to take the fight to the Mongs in Persia.'

'Like I said, not a bad idea...' muses Martin, as he paces around thinking and stroking his beard 'Not a bad idea at all'. He pauses a moment, then starts thinking out loud 'We'll need the bulk of our army to do this, we only need to leave just enough men to secure the peace here. We'll contact our spies from Persia to get a layout of the land where the enemy is camped. I don't believe we can surprise them completely, but we can attack them at their camp while they're preparing to come out and meet us. After the victory of the camp is established, word will go to the cities and more soldiers will come out to engage us. We'll retreat as if we thought that was all of them and we were victorious. We'll split the ranks in three, one up the middle and one on each flank far outside. The oncoming Mongs will attack the middle group thinking it is all of us. The flanks will return and close in on both of us as we fight to victory.'

'That's the kind of plan that I want to hear' states Justin, 'how soon can we prepare?'

'Today! Gather the chief men for a strategic meeting at headquarters. Put the word out immediately to get information from the spies in Persia. We need to know exactly where the Mong camp is and how many there are.'

So the plan is put into motion after the Crucifer leaders have agreed on the strategy to be executed. Soon they carry out their orders to organize the troops and prepare for deployment to Persia. After a few days time there are thousands of knightly figures traversing the desert followed by camels well laden with weapons and supplies and water. Spies are coming in every once in awhile with their reports of the situation in Persia. After many days of travel the massive army reaches the outer western area of Persia. Here they will not encounter any Persians yet and their presence will remain unknown. Justin meets with Martin at dusk as the men set camp.

'Finally the sun will set and we can cool off a little!'

'I've come to hate the damned sun out here in the desert!' replies Martin. 'I used to think it was so wonderful to be sunny all the time… I guess too much of anything turns it bad after awhile.'

'The spies report that the Mong camp is only a few miles east of here with only a few thousand soldiers. The rest of the army is miles away to the east outside the city.'

'Yes, I know. We need a day to rest and distribute all the weapons in preparation for the battle. We outnumber this group by thousands; I don't anticipate a long fight! But when the rest back at the city get word they will come out to attack us, and this will be the real test.'

'The guards are in place to let no one enter or leave the camp.'

'Very well, before sunrise the following morning we will march to the Mong camp and attack at daylight.'

A day of preparation passes quickly, then a short night of rest before arising before dawn to gather and march to the Mong camp. The Mongs have no word of the encroaching Crucifer army because they felt no reason for lookout or spies; after all they are the aggressors and assumed the Crucifers would prepare a defense at the Holy city. Some of the men are stirring at dawn and a few tend the horses. Another dry sunny day in the desert waiting for orders from Kublai has become the routine.

One of the Mong soldiers who went out to tend the horses raises his head thinking he hears something off in the distance. Another in the camp hears something also. In a split second the sound interprets itself to them; a very familiar sound… horses! Immediately there are shouts to arms all over the camp growing louder and louder. Men are scurrying back and forth trying to get into their gear and get to their horses. By now the whole western horizon is filled with dust and riders are coming at them at a fast pace. A few hundred Mongs are ready and go out to meet them while the rest try to get ready. The first group hardly slows the invaders down and they are cut down quickly. The general of the Mongs shouts a retreat, knowing this battle will be suicidal. All the camp is on horseback and ride away leaving the tents behind. The Crucifers pursue them trying to take as many as possible. The Mongs are very swift riders and shortly outrun the Crucifers. Martin sees this and gives the word to halt.

'I didn't expect them to run...' says Martin 'their reputation is for fierceness and tenacity.'

Justin replies 'They knew they didn't have a chance with our numbers, we should have attacked with less men!'

'Maybe so, but right now we're going to need all the men we have and then some! They're going to get the rest of their army and return... and not too long from now! Re-group the army and form camp, by tomorrow they will come at us. They're known for attacking straight on with their riders. I've changed the plan. We need to form ranks three sets deep. The first will be archers who after expiring all their arrows will return to the rear and prepare sword and shield. The second rank will still have two sets behind them to fall back to if they get into trouble. If we stop them, then we'll drive ahead.'

'And if we can't stop them, what then?' asks Justin.

'We disperse into the desert all different ways and meet up on the other side in a few days near the Holy city.'

'What's to stop them from hunting us down and slaughtering us when we split apart?'

Martin pauses a minute, then answers 'They will not split up like that, it will only cause confusion for them. They'll accept the victory and return. We can see they are not prepared to attack us in the Holy city yet. They'll want to re-group and plan their strategy for their next conquest.'

'If we get the advantage will we follow them to the city?'

'Of course we will, we'll cut them down outside and if they use the city for defense, we'll storm it and burn it to the ground.'

The Crucifer troops re-group and set camp. The cool evening sets in while each man eats, rests and prepares himself for tomorrow.

The desert sun awakens the troops with its brightness early in the morning. The night sentries return to get some sleep. There is no attack yet and the men have time to get into gear and prepare for the day ahead. Naturally there is a tension among them; it is a hard thing to wait for the battle to come to you. Too much time to think or let your mind wander to less focused thoughts. The leaders are among them trying to support their emotions and stimulate their bravery. Today they must be very, very brave for they will face the world's fiercest army. The word of the disperse maneuver is spread among them just in case, but no one acts like they will have to use it. As the morning moves to noontime the archers are set in front and the two ranks formed behind. It is getting hot very quickly.

'Sir, a scout is riding in and will be here momentarily with news of a sighting' says a commander. Martin walks out to greet him. In a few minutes the scout arrives.

'What news of the Mongs, did you see them out there?'

'Yes they are out there coming straight for us and not too far away… the good news is Kublai is not here. They say he has returned to his homeland ill. However, their new general is a great one also, his name is Hulegu and he now leads the horde.'

'Well done scout, return to the ranks' responds Martin. Then he turns to his commanders and says 'Ready the troops now for here they come. Archers prepare to fire at my word and only at my word, none too soon!'

A cloud of dust can be seen in the distance as the Mongs approach, thousands and thousands of them seeming to line the whole horizon with riders. Martin paces back and forth on his horse before the archers. He carefully eyes their distance and waits. Closer they come and he still waits, yet closer and still waiting he turns to face them. He raises his sword in the air and holds it high for a moment, then slashes it down and yells as loud as he can 'Fire now!' A rushing sound as a thousand birds taking off to flight fills the air and the arrows are so dense they form a shadow. Martin's timing is excellent as the first line of the charge rides right into arrow range. All over hundreds of Mongs and horses fall to arrows being hit with many more than one. The

19

force of the charge is slowed while the others behind them jump over the dead riders and their horses to get to the front.

Martin yells to the archers to fire all their arrows at will until they have no more then retreat to the rear and saddle up with sword and shield. By doing this many more Mong riders go down and the charge slows some more. Soon all are out of arrows and leave the front to the next group prepared for the battle that on Martin's command charge forward on their horses to meet the Mongs.

At first the clash is typical of the front line, but soon the swiftness and viciousness of the Mong soldiers and their bow skills shows through. The Crucifers are sweltering in the heat and their heavy armor and shields are slowing them down. As hard as they try they cannot match the speed and fierceness of these smaller but tough tenacious men. The first line of the Crucifers crumbles in defeat. The enemy comes upon the second line so fast that they are hardly prepared. Confusion sets in on the ranks, it's hard to tell who's who and the dust is blinding. Everything is happening so fast, they're not used to this level of accelerated aggression. They hold for a while but cannot keep up with the swiftness about them and start to fall by the hundreds. In a short time they are overwhelmed by the horde.

Martin yells the command to disperse, and hearing it the Crucifer soldiers immediately ride in every direction. Some of the Mongs follow individuals but most wait and look around for orders of what to do now. Their general gives the signal to regroup. The scattered Mongs leave the chase and return to the field to assemble again. After the dust settles they can see only small figures riding away all about the desert heading west. Hulegu comes to the front and says not to worry about these men now as he explains that they will finish this enemy when they attack Palestine in the near future.

THREE

Jerson is in the City of Peace doing errands and trading his wares as usual. There's a buzz among the locals about the Crucifers. He asks another trader what's the word going around. It seems the Crucifers have some sort of problem about concerns outside the city. It has been noticed that only enough of the army are here to keep order and the rest are away.

'I'm going to have to talk with some Crucifers and see if I can get anything out of them' he says to the other trader, 'watch my horse and stuff for awhile will you?'

'Sure' replies the trader.

So Jerson proceeds to a local tavern (that Crucifers are known to frequent) to get a drink and maybe some information. After he orders and takes his first long swig, he sizes up the crowd to see whom he should approach. There's a talkative fellow down the end with an audience of two or three men. He goes on down and stands by them listening and slowly blends in.

'It doesn't look good at all I tell ya... they're coming in one at a time from the desert, glad to be alive' the man is saying.

'Did you talk to them?' asks Jerson.

'No, but I saw a few... all beat looking and parched from the desert.'

'What do you think happened?'

'Oh I know what happened I sure do... but the rest aren't saying anything. They've been trounced out there somewhere by those damned Mongs is my bet. I heard that's where they were going, to Persia to attack them. We were left to keep the peace at home but not told about the plan for the troops leaving.'

'Isn't the general informing you men of the situation?' asks Jerson.

'Haven't heard yet but I'm sure he will sooner or later. I just wonder how close we are to being attacked.'

'Attacked by whom?' asks Jerson again.

'You ask a lot of questions, are you with the Crucifers or just another subversive native looking for trouble?'

'No, no... not looking for trouble, I'm just a trader wondering what's going on. If we're going to be attacked I'd sure like to know!' replies Jerson.

'Let me say this then... if I were you I'd stay within the city walls or go far from it in the mountains in the near future, maybe even days' states the man.

'You say it's the Mongs and they'll come from Persia?' asks another man.

'You heard what I think, I'll say no more…' says the man.

So Jerson finishes his drink and leaves. At the door he turns and waves to the men and thanks them for the conversation and backs out to the street. Right away he and a young maiden almost collide.

'Oh excuse me sir!' she exclaims.

'No, no… my fault' says Jerson 'I wasn't watching where I was going'. In an instant Jerson has taken this lady in with his eyes and his mind is swept up in awe. Her hair is fiery red and very wavy, her skin fair and white with little light brown patches all over like they had rained on her. Her eyes are magnificently blue and her lips full and lusciously red. He has to chuckle to himself as he sees her eyelids and eyebrows are red also. She starts to pick up some things she dropped so Jerson bends down to help.

'I'm so sorry I made you drop your things… my name is Jerson.'

'Don't feel bad Jerson; I've had worse mishaps! My name is Nicole.'

'Pleased to meet you Nicole, sorry it was this way though… where are you going?'

'Up to my place by the market.'

'I'll go with you, I left my horse and some wares in the market with a fellow trader, which I am also, I'm a trader and I travel with the nomads.'

'How interesting, you must know all this land then…you probably travel all over.'

'Yes I do but believe me it's not so interesting…and it gets dangerous sometimes. Where are you from?'

'My father is a Crucifer and brought me to see the Holy City when he came to liberate it from the Ishmaels. We're from Europe, our people are called Franks.'

'Your hair is red, are the Franks red headed?'

'Some of us are, the other Anglicans have more red heads.'

'It's so unusual out here. I've seen the yellow hairs also, fascinating. Some are very beautiful too. I think you're very beautiful with your red hair.'

'Oh thank you Jerson, you're so sweet' replies Nicole thinking to herself how handsome Jerson is with his tanned skin and dark hair and big dark eyes.

Soon they are at Nicole's home and stop to talk as they depart.

'I'd really like to see you again Nicole if that's all right with you?' says Jerson.

'I'd like that very much Jerson.'

'Well, how about going to the hills where the Savior walked outside the city tomorrow? We can bring some food and wine and sit under the trees.'

'That sounds good I'd like that. Will you come here to meet me?'

'Sure, I'll be here just before noon, see you then… goodbye'

'Bye'

Jerson returns to the market with each step bouncing off the ground, his arms swaying in rhythm and a large grin on his face that won't go away.

After he gets his horse and wares back from where he left them, he thanks the other trader and gives him a token for his trouble and returns to the nomad camp. Upon returning he sees Abul talking with the others so he approaches.

'It's the Mongs; they put the army to flight back in Persia. The Crucifer knights were scattered and are now returning to the city. There will be an invasion soon, we need to break camp immediately and go out into the mountains to be safe. Gather all by tomorrow, in the city and out and give them the word we will be leaving in a couple of days' he is saying.

'In a couple of days?' thinks Jerson 'I won't have time to see Nicole very much, I'll have to ride into town every now and then… well, at least there's tomorrow.'

'Jerson! Hey Jerson' shouts Albert.

'Albert, what's going on?' says Jerson dismounting to greet his friend.

Albert starts right in… 'All these Crucifers are straggling back to the city from the desert; the word is they were scattered by the Mongs in Persia. There aren't many casualties though because they weren't chased. The Mongs returned to their city but it looks like they will come this way very soon.'

'I know, I heard Abul talking. Looks like we're headed for the mountains for awhile!'

So Jerson and Albert talk some more and go about their daily chores and ready themselves for the evening. Jerson goes to his tent with one thing on his mind, seeing Nicole tomorrow. It is hard to sleep with the anticipation of tomorrow bubbling in his mind. But soon without realizing it he has dozed off and slept the night away. The sun is up and doves are cooing, the animals are stirring and a cool breeze is blowing through the tent. Jerson gets up and goes about the morning chores and gets breakfast and tends the animals. It seems like no time at all until noon. Now he is merrily on his way to Nicole's place. As he approaches he notices a man by the door talking with Nicole.

'Hello Nicole' says Jerson.

'Hello Jerson, this is my father Bertrand, he stopped by to see me this morning.'

'Hello sir' says Jerson.

'Jerson is it?' says the man.

Bertrand sizes up Jerson with his eyes and is little impressed. He begins the conversation.

'I understand you are a nomad trader?'

'Yes I am' answers Jerson.

'What do you think of our noble undertaking here in this land?'

'I don't think much about it because you were in control when we arrived and we accepted and respect your rule as we do wherever we are welcome and set camp.'

'Don't you appreciate your liberation from these Philistines?'

Jerson pauses sensing an argument, then answers 'I don't think they're all Philistines anymore.'

'For us they are all Philistines or Covenants responsible for the death of the Savior.'

'The death of the Savior was predetermined by God to be the sacrifice for the sins of the world.'

'Are you preaching to me young man?' asks Bertrand pompously.

'No, just stating the word we know from the Loways who came from the original apostles teachings.'

'I sense you don't approve of the army of God.'

'If you mean the Crucifers are the army of God I'm afraid I don't see it that way.'

'Then how do you see it young man?' asks Bertrand cynically.

'Since the time of the Savior, it is said we don't wrestle with flesh and blood but with principalities and powers that try to dissuade us from our faith. The army of God is the angels that the Savior said he could call but did not because his suffering was his purpose here to save us.'

'Then who would save you from these Philistines that had control of the holy city and the tomb of the Savior? Our faith is not in the sky, but here and now doing the will of God and establishing his church in an unholy world.'

'By means of violence and cruelty?' asks Jerson sternly.

'By means of the power of God vested in us to forge his will on unbelievers who will be damned if we do not.'

'Everything in the world goes according to God's will, even the Savior said to those who held him they could not have the power to do so but it be given to them of God. It was even God's will to harden the heart of Pharaoh in the old days to not let the Covenants go from Egypt. Pharaoh did God's will but I hardly think he was in God's favor!'

'Are you saying we are not in God's favor boy! I'll gladly send you to him so you can ask directly!'

'No, no I'm not saying that! You wouldn't be victorious without it being the will of God. I'm just examining the spirit of the thing.' Responds Jerson cautiously. Then he goes on:

'It just seems the original teachings are more peaceful.'

'Are you another Philistine lover? Isn't it more peaceful now since we've conquered?'

'Yes I suppose it is.' Responds Jerson realizing there is no settling these opposing views.

'Now, now you two, no politics today' says Nicole 'Jerson and I are going to walk into the hills and have lunch there' she says to her father. 'And Jerson, I've brought some dried fish and bread and dates.'

29

'Sounds good' says Jerson anxious to leave the presence of her father. They say their goodbyes and Jerson and Nicole are on their way.

They spend most of the afternoon conversing in the splendor of this beautiful day. Jerson is quite taken with this young lady and thoughts of fanciful romance drift through his head. Nicole is at ease with this new friend and enjoys his company and engaging but entertaining conversation. Evening draws near so they both agree it's time to return home. At Nicole's place they stop to say good evening.

'Oh Jerson what a great time I had this afternoon, thanks so much for taking me.'

'The pleasure is all mine; I thought the afternoon would never end! Let's do some more things together, I promise I'll find the time.'

'Sure, that sounds good now that you know where to find me. So, I'll be seeing you later then.'

'Good evening Nicole, 'till next time.'

Nicole enters her house when she notices someone there. She immediately recognizes her father.

'Father, you came over again.'

'Yes I did, just to see how my baby's doing? I don't mean to pry but you know I worry about you in this strange land. How did things go with that young man?'

'Jerson? He's sweet and friendly and quite innocent.'

'He's also a nomad, maybe a heathen!'

'No, he follows the teachings of the Loways…'

'The Loways! Who the hell are they anyhow? What do they know of the Savior? They're not even in the church!'

'I don't know father but he seems to know the Savior.'

'What does he know? That the way is low? The way is low, with suffering for your sins and duty to the church! He doesn't seem like he's suffering much for his and he does not belong to the church.'

'He's a nice man father and a friend, don't worry, I don't have romantic interests with him.'

'Good. Find a good young knight for that, a noble young man who will take you back home in honor and care for you.'

'Good night father!'

Bertrand grumps and takes the queue from Nicole that it's time to leave.

FOUR

Martin has returned to the City of Peace and confers with those he left in charge after his first engagement with the Mongs. The mood is somber and apprehensive. Justin speaks:

'The horde is more aggressive and powerful than any of us ever thought. Their speed is baffling and their riding and bow skills unmatched by any army in existence. We were lucky to flee with our lives. The next conflict with them will be only worse for us, I'm sure the men are very demoralized now. We need a plan and we need help and very soon.'

'First gather the knights back together' is Martin's reply 'we must encourage them all to gain back some confidence.'

'How many casualties?' asks one of the other leaders.

'We don't know yet, but we were able to flee and they didn't pursue us very far, so our casualties were mostly those who fell in the conflict. I'd say maybe a quarter of us or less has been lost' states Martin.

After talking more of the battle and defeat, the leaders disperse and round up all the knights to gather in the Holy City once more. The chore is easy because all the scattered knights are seeking rest from the elements and desire to be back at camp where there's food and water. Inside the city many knights have shown up on their own accord. A couple of days pass and a strategic meeting is held at the headquarters of the camp. Martin takes charge and begins to speak.

'You all know why we're here and you all know our situation. I don't feel we can conquer these damn Mongs by ourselves. I want to hear about substantial allies we can call upon without losing face and appearing weak and on the run. The people don't know of the real defeat we've suffered, only rumors. We need to appear strong and act like we came back this way purposely as a strategy to regroup. Tell the people it's what we intended to do and that we chose to face the invaders here should they come. So, what do we have?'

Argyle, one of the knight's leaders speaks up.

'We have knowledge of a Turkish slave class of riding warriors called Mamluks being trained in Egypt by the sultan Baybars. He excels on the battlefield much like Ghengis did and trains on the polo fields with an elite corps of these Mamluks whose skills are second to none. They are subject to the great leader Qutuz. Qutuz is worried for the Ishmaelites all over this land that the Mongs may conquer them. He follows the teaching of not waiting for the battle to come to you but taking it to the camp of the enemy.'

'Very good' says Martin 'but so far away, if we're attacked any time soon they will not make it here in time. Send word to them that we will need them in the fight against the Mongs but they must come right away because we are in danger of attack.'

Justin speaks up also:

'The nomads will be leaving for the mountains. The Ishmaelites and Covenants are willing to fight with us because of the common threat to the city. We gave the word to sign in at the camp and already many of them are preparing with us for the attack.'

The Crucifers begin their preparation for an attack while the nomads are preparing to leave the city. Nicole goes to see Jerson at the nomad camp because she has news from her father of an impending attack. Upon arriving she is asked what her business is there by Abul. She explains she is looking for Jerson the trader she has recently befriended in town. Abul thinks to himself that here is a beautiful young lady looking for the man he has plans with for one of his daughters, although he hasn't told anyone especially Jerson. He doesn't like this but instead of sending her off he shows her where Jerson's tent is. As she approaches Jerson comes walking out of the entrance.

'Hello Jerson' she says 'an old gray bearded man called Abul showed me where your tent is.'

'Nicole!' says Jerson surprisingly 'what are you doing here?'

'I wanted to come and tell you of the news my father told me...'

Jerson interrupts 'No matter, I'm glad you're here to see me for whatever reason.'

About this time comes Albert walking by noticing a beautiful young lady with Jerson.

'Jerson, how are you?' he says.

'Albert, fine and you?'

'Good, what's the word for today and who is this beautiful lady might I ask?'

'Oh, this is my friend Nicole. Her father is a Crucifer knight of some standing. She was just about to tell me some news.'

'Hello Nicole my name is Albert'

Nicole looks deeply into Albert's eyes, a look that causes a little twinge of jealousy in Jerson's heart. Albert returns the gaze as she speaks:

'Hello Albert, are you a Frank?'

'Why yes I am, and you?'

'Yes, I am also. Are you a Crucifer too?'

'That's a long story... let's just say I know a lot about them. Right now I'm a nomad like Jerson. What news do you have?'

'My father says we're preparing for a Mong invasion to take place very soon.'

Jerson responds first; 'I knew it; we've heard the rumors and the nomads are leaving for the mountains. I was coming over to see you and tell you about it Nicole.'

'Are you staying in the city?' asks Albert of Nicole.

'I have no choice, I won't abandon my father and the Crucifers will protect the city.'

'I hope so, we hear these Mongs are an awfully strong army' says Jerson.

'So Nicole, you'll have to tell me where you're from, I may know it from my homeland' says Albert. Nicole gladly responds as the two go on about their past and their homeland together. Jerson excuses himself, kind of being ignored anyhow, and goes about preparing for the move. Albert and Nicole are dreamily reminiscing about many places they've both been to and many things they miss and have done back home as they walk off together.

The next day finds Jerson still preparing to leave with the nomads and Albert preparing also but a little behind since he spent yesterday almost entirely with Nicole. As their paths cross again Albert hails Jerson.

'Hey Jerson!'

'Albert, how are you doing?'

'Catching up on the move, I spent the whole day talking with Nicole yesterday. She's quite a girl.'

Jerson's heart sinks a little at the news.

'Really…'

'Yeah, she says you've been a good friend… like having a brother out here in this uncertain land.'

'Really…'

'I'll tell you, I can't help falling for her, and don't you think she's beautiful?'

'Yes, I do… she is beautiful.'

'We kissed when we left. Oh what a kiss, you know those long sweet ones?'

'Yeah…' stammers Jerson not wanting to hear any more.

'Well I'm going to see her again today after I get some work done here.'

'What? Her father's a Crucifer! What if someone recognizes you?'

'I'll be careful, and I don't have to see her father.'

Jerson is more concerned about Albert now than worrying about his feelings for Nicole being hurt. He knows this is risky behavior and Albert may not be thinking clearly at this time. He also knows he's not going to stop Albert from seeing her now. He still feels he's got to try.

'Albert, listen, you're being a little nuts right now. You shouldn't leave the security of the nomads and especially to go around Crucifers again! They kill deserters don't they? Probably torture them first! You can't take that risk.'

'Oh don't worry so much Jerson, the area she lives in is mostly Ishmaels and the Crucifers aren't around there. I'll watch out for her father in case he comes around. Everyone else will see me as a nomad.'

'You'd better really watch out… I mean every second.'

'Don't worry!'

So Albert finishes his work in a short while and merrily goes on his way to see Nicole. Of course the two begin to get very close in a short period of time. Each day until he is ready to leave he visits her. Jerson decides to just stay out of it; it only makes his heart ache anyhow. The nomads are beginning to leave town now but Albert stays on awhile longer confident he will catch up to them later. Jerson decides to leave with the nomads.

Today again Albert is on his way to Nicole's. As he nears her neighborhood a Crucifer passing through happens to notice him. Albert had let the hood of his robe fall back on his head too much revealing his pale skin. Not the skin of the natives thinks the soldier. He reports his finding to his superior Algernon who is a crude sadistic man hating his fate here in this desert land. Algernon is not a high-ranking officer, just a sergeant of a small group. He despises the upper command seeing himself just as qualified but never promoted to their level. He rarely consults them and usually does what he decides is best to do. His orders are to apprehend this man and whoever is with him.

As Albert and Nicole are returning from a walk in the countryside this Crucifer soldier with drawn sword suddenly stops them. Albert's heart sinks in his chest and he thinks 'Oh my God don't let this happen' knowing his fate if he is caught. Nicole asks what's going on and states that her father is a high-ranking Crucifer officer. The soldier does not know Nicole's father and brings them to Algernon. There are so many officers that

Algernon doesn't recognize Nicole's father's name either. The soldier takes Algernon aside and says:

'Sir, what if the girl's statement is true and her father is who she says?'

'She's just been arrested; she'll say anything to get free! It's the man I'm concerned about. Let's find out what his story is.'

Algernon questions Albert about who he is and what he is doing here. Albert's story of being a nomad and trader doesn't sit well with Algernon. He has Nicole kept quiet during the inquisition.

'A nomad? I don't think so! You're European, look at your skin. How do you know our language so well?'

'I'm not denying being European' says Albert 'I'm here to trade…'

'There aren't any European traders here since we've taken control. We do all the trading. I'm thinking at your age and build you were a fine Crucifer soldier at one point.'

Albert denies this and gives no more information to Algernon.

'It looks like we need to do a little extraction' says Algernon 'tie them and bring them with me to the chamber.'

The soldier ties them and prods them to follow Algernon downstairs to a torture chamber. Albert is sweating a little and his heart is in his throat knowing what's to come. Nicole is very worried now and less confident her father's influence will save them from this terrible situation. She scolds Algernon in her father's name about what she sees about to happen here but he only slaps her across the face and shoves her into a chair and gags her. Albert can do nothing. Algernon has the soldier secure Albert on a rack and orders him to wait outside the closed door and guard them.

Now the sordid affair of questions and pain begins. Albert denies being a Crucifer time and time again as Nicole tries to scream through the gag each time Algernon initiates pain. Tears are streaming down Nicole's face and she can hardly stand to hear Albert's screams finally brought about after heroically suffering quietly for so long. Still he will not cooperate with Algernon.

Algernon backs off for a little bit and begins eyeing Nicole. Albert knows the look and winces at the thought. He can't help blurt out: 'Leave her alone you filthy bastard!'

'Oh, so this is where the nerve is! I should have known. It's been a long, long time since I've had a woman… well other than these dark pigs in the city hardly women at all. Beautiful white skin and gorgeous red hair…' He rips the upper half of the garment from Nicole's body.

'Now that's a sight to behold!'

'You goddamn swine, you leave her alone…' yells Albert.

At this Algernon tears away the rest of Nicole's garment. Albert is almost berserk with rage and rants at Algernon incessantly. Algernon grabs his dagger and holds it to Albert's throat and says 'I can't enjoy this with all your damned yelling' and coolly runs it across and steps back as the blood spurts out on the floor. Albert's torture is over. Nicole slumps down with a heart-wrenching groan. Algernon prepares himself to take his pleasure with Nicole.

While this was happening, unbeknownst to Algernon the soldier at the door decided this was not right and left to get an officer to check out this situation. The officer Andre, when told of the girl's story, bolted up immediately knowing the name of her father. The two have returned to the chamber and burst in on Algernon just beginning to rape Nicole. No explanation is needed for Andre as the scene he is witnessing instantly outrages him. Algernon can barely get to his feet before Andre says 'you bloody bastard' and runs him through with his sword. Andre unties Nicole who is limp with shock and covers her with his own cape. He orders the soldier to take Albert off the rack and try to identify him with the other soldiers. He also orders the body of Algernon to be brought to the hall where he knows Nicole's father is. When other soldiers come he leaves with the one's carrying Algernon.

As they enter the hall Bertrand noticing Nicole rises from his chair. Before he can ask for an explanation Andre speaks up.

'Sir Bertrand, I was called to a questionable situation by this soldier and found this bastard in a torture chamber raping your bound daughter, in my rage at this scene I ran him through with my sword. Here he is…' The soldiers throw Algernon's body on the floor.

Bertrand comes down and puts his arms around Nicole and holds her closely.

41

'Is this true my dear?'

'Yes father... but Algernon also tortured a young man who was becoming my lover.'

'I commend your action Andre; this will be viewed as a deed of swift deserving justice. The young man I cannot speak for. I'm sorry Nicole, we'll have to find out who he is and bury him.'

At this time a few more soldiers come in, one of them says:

'Sir Bertrand, we've identified the man in the chamber. He is Albert St. Onge, a deserter missing for some time.'

Bertrand turns to Nicole and says:

'I'm sorry Nicole; I will say no more of this man nor your involvement with him. I need to know nothing more, I just want you to get over your grief and recover from all this. I'm putting Andre to your charge and I will make arrangements for you to return home to Europe with him immediately.'

'As you wish Sir' says Andre with a bow. Slowly everyone goes about clearing the room and Bertrand has Andre take Nicole to her flat to clean up and rest.

Jerson is wondering about Albert and Nicole so much that he decides to ride into town and see if he can find out how they're doing. The first place to check will be Nicole's flat. When he gets there she is not home, so he tethers his horse to a pole and waits awhile sitting out front thinking Nicole may return home at any time.

Nicole and Andre are coming up the street when she gets a glimpse of Jerson sitting outside prompting her to run up the street calling his name.

'Jerson, Jerson…'

'Nicole…' he says puzzled by the man with her.

Nicole hugs him heartily and still holding on begins the tale.

'This is Andre; my father put me in his care. Oh Jerson Albert is dead, dead…' sobs Nicole.

'No, no, no… what happened?'

Nicole explains everything as best she can between sobs as Jerson keeps thinking 'damn it I knew it, I knew he might get caught!' She also explains that she will be leaving for home with Andre very soon. This news is agreeable to Jerson; he knows it's best for her. He also knows he has to let her go in his heart; she didn't feel for him the way he did for her. He sees Andre is a handsome man and an honorable knight. Only a little time together will probably yield some affection from Nicole, and if he has any sense he will return it. Soon Jerson is ready to leave to let Nicole clean up and rest. He suggests he come by tomorrow to say good-bye. She agrees and enters her flat with Andre who will camp out in the living room and remain at her side from now until they are safely home.

In the morning Jerson comes by as promised and they say their good-byes in good spirits with many hugs, then Jerson is on his way back to the nomads.

FIVE

It's been awhile now since Nicole has left the country and Bertrand is more at ease. But there is a new worry for him to wrestle with as he takes his place in the ranks waiting for whatever the day's orders bring. There are rumors of a Mong invasion of the Holy City, very serious rumors sounding more like truth every day. Martin is feeling the pressure to let out some information about this but not panic the people. He decides to let the troops know and prepare them to defend the city, the people will find out about it by word of mouth when someone talks, and Martin well knows that someone will always talk. He informs Justin with the other leaders that an attack is imminent and to order their men to prepare to defend the city. Justin waits for the others to leave and speaks with Martin privately.

'So, you're sure they're coming?'

'I'm surprised they're not here yet' replies Martin.

'What will we do? We took a beating in the desert, how can we stop them here?'

'I don't believe we can… that's why I've prepared a retreat.'

'That's not very heartening Martin…'

'It's between you and I old friend, don't let it out to the men that I feel this way; we'll fight our best to save this place, but not to the last man. When it looks as if they will prevail, we will lead the men out by the north west because I believe they will come in through the south east side. They probably won't follow because they'll want to secure the city. We will live to fight again another time.'

'You have my word… actually I believe this is a good plan' confesses Justin.

Martin's timing is good and not a moment too soon for Mong spies have been spotted in the area outside the city. Fear has spread among those outside the city and they are returning rapidly for the protection of the city walls. The word has spread like wildfire throughout as the Crucifers man the walls to face the invaders. Soon everyone is inside and the gates are shut and locked. Now it's kind of peaceful all around and quiet as the wait begins. It isn't a long wait, maybe an hour before the first sightings come in.

The Mong army is here and have lined up across the ridge on top of the Mount of Olives facing the Holy City.

'How ironic…' states Martin 'they came from the east across the Judea Wilderness like the savior did to the Mount of Olives to enter the Holy City!' then he makes the call to battle ready.

45

'I wish the savior was returning on the mount today!' exclaims Martin 'but I hardly think so, God help us all…'

The Mongs have begun the attack with soldiers riding in shooting torrents of arrows at the men on the walls and behind the walls. They continue back and forth before the walls shooting arrows and yelling while the rest make their way down from the mount until they're all there. The Crucifers have been returning fire as well and the casualties begin to mount on both sides. As expected, the ladders are brought forth and the battering rams for the gates too. Soon the Mongs are climbing up to face the Crucifers hand-to-hand on the walls. Things are stable for a short while as the Crucifers use the advantage of the wall to fight back the intruders. The gates are holding so far. But the tenacity of the Mong army is becoming very apparent as it swarms at the wall without a break and hammers away at the gates unceasingly. All too soon it is too much for the Crucifers and the gates to hold. Like a great tide they pour over the wall all at once and cut down the retreating Crucifers mercilessly. When the gate gives way they rush in fervently attacking all in their path as they charge. Martin has already backed to the north gate and gives word for the Crucifers to retreat out of the city. As the front line fights on the rest go through the gate or over the wall until all the surviving Crucifers are out of the city heading across the northland rapidly. The Mongs do not chase but remain and relish their victory in the city. As before, Hulegu knows confidently that he can attack them out there at a later time and finish them.

Out in the wilderness the Crucifer soldiers are scattering everywhere, but they soon realize they aren't being pursued. As they wander about now, Martin gives the order:

'Regroup all the men, we're heading north east to the plain by the sea.'

So the leaders round up all the fleeing army into one group, and order is restored and some shreds of dignity remain from this resounding defeat.

'Where are the Mamluks? If they were here we'd fare a lot better' asks Justin.

'They've started to come north from Egypt is the word, but still a long way off.'

'Will they attack the city?'

'I don't know, they're not very interested in us. Their allegiance is to the Ishmaels and therefore they plan their attack to the advantage of the whole country. Sooner or later they will try to retake the City of Peace.'

'I don't like it at all and didn't like it from the beginning!' states Justin 'I feel this is our last stand in this part of the world. The Mongs want to defeat us, and ultimately so do the Ishmaels. And now we're out in the open and vulnerable to all. Either way we have a great enemy to deal with, the Mamluks will be just as impossible to defeat as the Mongs!'

'You sound defeated already Justin!'

'Just a realist I guess… you know I will fight to the death… but I won't fool myself, I always try to know the strength of my enemy.'

'Don't let any of this "realism" out to anybody… we need to build morale in the troops. The word will be that the Mamluks will help us defeat the Mongs and re-establish our rule in the land.'

SIX

It is weeks later and Jerson has been camping out under the stars with his tribe of nomads far from the Holy city. His mind wanders less now about Nicole and Albert. Though when he does think of them there is still a lump in his throat. However there is another person to think about now, Sofia, who is Abul's daughter. When Abul first introduced them she was just a child. Yet she is now fully grown and quite beautiful in the nomad look but Jerson is hardly swept away by her. She is quiet and shy and holds Jerson in great admiration. She knows him thoroughly because he has been such a popular figure with the nomads and her father would always tell her what he was up to. There only was and still is Jerson in her desires. Abul walks out of his tent and goes up to Jerson who is staring out into the heavens.

'Do you see your destiny in those stars Jerson?' he asks.

'No I don't, just admiring the beauty of the night.'

'Yes, yes… many nights have I gazed at them wondering, hoping, praying.'

49

'Did they form your destiny Abul?'

'No, no of course not… the Savior did that you know. They only give signs, like the one at his birth to the kings seeking him.'

'Well, no signs for me tonight…' sighs Jerson.

'No? Well maybe some advice then.'

'Sure'

'You're a fine man Jerson, a fine man. Only you're going past the marrying age of most of us. You should be thinking of a family and fathering children. You've done very well trading and have the means to support a family. You're highly respected in our tribe and could have any one of the available women. But gladly to me you have shown no interest in them. I say this because I would be very proud to have a son like you. I would like you to consider my daughter Sofia, the most beautiful I have fathered in my time on this earth. She thinks of no one but you Jerson, and this from childhood! It is a great comfort to have such a woman, and hard for most men to find. Her devotion will be like a well that is always full to draw from. She will gladly bear your children, and many too.'

'Oh I don't know Abul…' interrupts Jerson 'I have great respect for you and would gladly do the things you suggest that are good, but with the recent events it's hard for me to think of this now.'

'Just talk with her sometimes, real conversation instead of just being nice and polite. Give her some time and see how you feel about her then.'

'I will Abul, but I can't promise you anything.'

'I'm not asking any promises Jerson, just some of your time.'

'That I can do… thanks for the talk, I think I'll go to sleep soon, good night Abul.'

'Good night Jerson.'

Abul walks back to his tent with a broad smile across his face, Jerson goes to his tent thinking of Sofia. She is nice to look at even though her hair and skin are darker than the Europeans like Nicole. He supposes he just didn't notice her because she was just a common nomad like he is. Now that he thinks of her as he would an available woman, she is very beautiful after all.

The next day finds Jerson talking with Sofia as promised. The conversation is natural and unforced, she floats on his every word and responds with the best timing so easily. Their movements are fluid and free of clumsiness leaving Jerson to wonder why he had not taken time with her before. He feels so comfortable with her now, a comfort that goes down to his soul and refreshes him. He can feel the love she has for him warm and sincere and it makes him feel a little wanting with his own since he hadn't loved her until this day. And this day is rapidly convincing him that he indeed needs to love her. Although his mind is starting to convince him his heart is far out in front as he feels his spirit starting to soar. But before he can put the words together for Sofia, riders galloping furiously towards them capture their attention. One stops and dismounts as the others go on.

'You'd better get your things and flee this area now, you're too close to the Holy city. The Mongs have invaded and driven out the Crucifers. They're fleeing into northern Palestine now. If you don't want to be captured you'd better go there too.'

'Thank you for warning us' shouts Jerson as the rider goes off after the others.

Sofia and Jerson say quick good-byes and return to their tents to prepare to leave. Already Abul is out and about gathering the nomads who are ready and prodding the others to make haste. Soon the whole camp is ready and on Abul's lead begins to ride out. Camels, horses, sheep, cattle and carts are stirring up large dust clouds as they go. The trip will take many days but this is life as usual for nomadic people who often wander long distances on short notice. Jerson rides up to Abul and asks:

'Where are we going?'

'To the northern plain of Palestine to be under the protection of Crucifers' replies Abul.

'Protection? If they can't hold the Holy city how can they protect us?'

'Well, maybe not protection but they can be a buffer between the Mongs and us. Then we can be among the rest of the people of this land.'

So the nomads leave the area and head northwest to the plains and the sea. Many days later they arrive at a camp of Ishmaels who welcome them. They set camp here also. Usual greetings are made as all settle down and find a place to pitch their tents.

The Ishmaels and nomads have long been friends even though the nomads are also friends with the Covenants, who have been at odds with the Ishmaels for centuries. When everyone is settled Abul takes Jerson to speak with the Ishmael leader Ali Al-Fulani.

After the usual respects are exchanged they begin to converse:

'You know the Mongs have taken the Holy City?' asks Abul.

'Yes, we have had word of it. We were expecting them for some time since they conquered Persia' replies Ali.

'What will we do now? They may decide to come out after us in the rest of the land.'

'Yes we're hoping they will do this.'

'Hoping they will do this?' exclaims Abul 'why would you do that?'

'They do not know of Qutuz on his way from Egypt probably in Palestine already. They will look for Crucifers to defeat totally but he will come up and surprise them.'

'I see, but is he powerful enough to do this?'

'He commands Baybars, a ruthless leader of a mounted corps of exceptional warriors much like the Mongs. Along with his troops and volunteers from all of Palestine they number 120,000 men'

'Very formidable indeed, this news is strengthening my nerves and confidence to stay in this land and to see the Mongs finally stopped!'

The situation is changing back in the Holy City. There is bad news for the Mongs; back home their emperor Kublai has died. This has always been a weakness historically for them, and again it strikes the present leader Hulegu. He withdraws almost his entire army to return home for the funeral of Kublai and leaves only a minor force of 15,000 to watch the horizon. Keda is in charge of them with 10,000 allies. Still confident in their strength and skills, Keda prepares to route the Covenants from the land. He has reports that they have fled northwest almost to the sea. He sends his troops west at first with plans to go up the plains and sweep out the Covenants and force them to retreat with the sea at their backs. The Mongs stop at a watering hole area called Ain Julut to refresh themselves and their steeds. They decide to camp here for a short while and regroup the troops and verify the current plan of attack.

The word gets to the Ishmaels where Jerson and the nomads are that just to the south at Ain Julut the Mongs have set camp. Ali Al-Fulani smiles at hearing the news. Jerson however is a little beside himself when he hears it. He rushes up to Abul who is talking with Ali and interrupts:

'Abul… My god! The Mongs are out here already just south of us… what are we going to do?'

'Well Jerson, you can watch if you want…'

'Watch? Watch what? We need to get the hell out of here!'

'Fate is about to play a cruel game on the Mongs and the Crucifers Jerson. While the Mongs are camped out at Ain Julut, just to the south of them is an army of 120,000 men including a specially trained group as fierce or even fiercer than the Mongs themselves. The Mongs know nothing of this because their attention is focused north and they do not have spies to the south. The local Ishmaels are relieved by this army and will not divulge information about it to a soul. The sultan Baybars has plans to rid the land of the Crucifers as well and turn it back over to the Ishmaels. If you want to watch you can ride with Ali and myself to Ain Julut.'

'This is amazing… this ought to be a good one! I'll go with you.'

SEVEN

It's taken a night and a day's ride to get to Ain Julut but the three arrive and stop at a hill just far enough away not to be detected. Here they can see that nothing has happened so far. In the distance are the tents and horses of the Mongs surrounding the watering hole. They knew they couldn't get to it when they got here so all of them have brought water for themselves and their horses. As it turns out they've arrived uncannily at the same time a large cloud of dust appears on the southern horizon.

'Strange… it looks as though the Mong numbers have diminished, this is not the amount of men they had at the Holy City, much more were there, much more!' states Abul.

'Look' says Jerson 'to the south… that cloud must be Qutuz and his army coming.'

'Our timing couldn't have been better' says Ali 'today judgment will arrive for the Mongs!'

The Mongs have noticed the cloud also and begin to assemble the troops as they send some out to investigate. Shortly they return a little stunned with the news of a great army coming towards them from the south. Keda shouts the command to set the troops for battle. There is no strategy for position so they take the time to line up across the land many deep and prepare to face the oncoming charge right here. By now the advancing army is within sight, and if it had been any other people but the Mongs they most likely would have retreated because now it has become apparent that they are clearly outnumbered.

The first wall of men and horses slam into each other with such furor that it can be heard loudly all the way out to where Jerson, Abul and Ali are watching. For a time the battle rages on in one place with both sides suffering many casualties. There is no appearance of advantage yet. It goes on and on until suddenly the attacking army retreats back to some hills. This draws the Mongs in because they think they have taken the advantage and they charge after them. When they catch up to the fleeing army they are shocked by the sight of troops coming out of the hills at them on both sides. The retreat was a fake. The army before them stops retreating and turns to face them. Instead of disheartening the men, the seriousness of the situation only makes the Mongs fight more fiercely. They soon gain momentum and stop the oncoming surge of the enemy and they nearly break through the left flank. But seeing this weakness in his assault, Qutuz shouts "Islamah! Islamah!" many times and rallies his troops behind him with renewed spirit and vigor to take the victory from the Mongs and they overwhelm them. It takes a little time but Qutuz, Baybars and their fighting men kill all of the Mongs. This day is become the first time ever that the Mong army or any part of it has suffered defeat.

'We are blessed to have witnessed this great event' says Ali after it is clearly over 'let's go greet the victorious Qutuz and Baybars.'

So the three go on down to the watering hole cheering and waving at the joyous men all about them. Ali congratulates the leaders and is told by Baybars that he is going north to drive out the Franks once and for all from the land. Ali praises him and his god and gives him charge of any of his men he may need when they get to Ali's camp since the three will be returning that way with Baybars' army.

Now at the camp, Jerson takes leave of Ali and Abul and seeks out Sofia. When he finds her he tells her of the great battle he witnessed and the defeat of the Mongs. He also goes on about the fate of the Crucifers who will finally be forced out of the land for good. Sofia hangs on every word and her heart is reassured for the future now being free of the two great oppressors almost at the same time. But it is the anticipation of the future with Jerson that worries her now.

'So now I can rest a lot easier' says Jerson 'the Holy City will be a good trading place free of the Crucifers and maybe at last there will be somewhat of a peace in the land.'

This is not much consolation for Sofia's worries.

'I'm tired of traveling all around all the time. Maybe I should settle outside the city for a while, I know Abul will bring the nomads back now that we have freedom under Ishmael rule. I like staying with you people you know.'

It's getting a little better for Sofia now.

'Actually I was thinking a lot about you and me Sofia, I mean spending some time together... you know?'

It's getting a lot better for Sofia now.

'Would you like to do some things together Sofia? I'd like to get to know you a lot more...'

'I'd love to Jerson' she says getting closer.

'You know what I'm trying to say then?'

'Yes, I think I do...'

Jerson takes her hand and looks into her eyes, his heart beating a little harder with anticipation. Sofia puts her arm up and around his shoulder so Jerson responds by putting his arms around her waist and drawing her near. Sofia looks up at him with love in her eyes and Jerson's heart is melted, so he slowly leans towards her and kisses her gently on the lips. Sofia's response is warm and gentle as they both press a little harder. Neither wants to stop but they are outside and this sort of behavior is better kept in the tent away from prying eyes. But it is too late for one set of eyes, those of Abul who has witnessed the kiss and goes to his tent dancing!

A few months later the nomads are safely settled outside the city and trading, herding and rearing their animals. Life is good.

Jerson imagines the Savior smiling down upon him and finally feels at home. His business is good and his tent full. Everything is back to normal only better. But still there is one thing that remains to be done, yes the crowning jewel of this completed adventure he thinks... wedding plans with Sofia!

BAITING THE SYSTEM

ONE

The big city is ripe for the chase. Aggressive drivers are pushing everyone to move faster and jerking in and out of any opening in the traffic. One is in such a rush that he veers out onto the shoulder to pass and accelerates right through a red light. A cruising police car notices this action and starts to follow.

The officer puts his lights and siren on to pull the car over. The car does not pull over but speeds up heading towards an on-ramp to the freeway. The officer radios in that he is in pursuit of a reckless driver in a red Mazda entering the 2nd Avenue on-ramp east bound. The traffic is light so he can follow right behind the car accelerating with it as he chases it down the freeway. Soon they're both doing over 100 miles per hour but the officer is keeping up with him. After a few miles another police cruiser pulls onto the freeway ahead of them. Seeing this the suspect moves to the outside lane and passes it with the first officer still following close behind. The second cruiser pulls up behind the first in the chase. Soon the three of them are coming up on a driver in the lane doing the speed limit. The Mazda is not slowing but is giving a few horn blasts as the car moves out of the lane. This a temporary remedy because soon they are up to another car in the lane. This time the suspect cuts back to the middle lane and with the officer following passes the car. The traffic is picking up ahead. The Mazda begins to weave in and out of the 3 lanes and the first officer stays with him but the second cannot because he's almost side swiping the cars they're passing not having enough length of highway between them.

The suspect decides to get off the freeway and makes a reckless turn from the outside lane to the off-ramp. The first officer follows with tires squealing and skidding but makes it off also. The second officer cannot make it and goes on to the next exit. The Mazda is still doing about 60 mph as it shoots up the ramp and onto the road running parallel. The car ahead is going way too slow and the Mazda is on him as if out of nowhere. The suspect rear ends the car at its right rear bumper and sends it off the road spinning in to the cyclone fence. This hasn't damaged the Mazda much because it had the momentum and basically drove the car off sustaining only broken lights and a dent. The officer stays right behind the Mazda trying to radio in help for the crash victim. As they go a few more miles another police cruiser comes darting out on the road they're racing down. The Mazda is quick to react and side swipes the car but gets out ahead. Still the first officer is right behind.

The intersection of Access Lane (the road the police cars and Mazda are racing down) and Industry Boulevard is very busy. There's a stop sign there on Access Lane because of crossing two-lane oncoming traffic that does not have to stop. This could be a catastrophic intersection for a chase… and it's about to be that way!

A Ford Explorer followed by an 18-wheeler semi-truck is coming down the road at about 50 mph.

The timing couldn't be worse. It's become very eerie for the pursuing officer because as soon as he realizes the situation time seems to slow down. Instinctively his foot goes to the brake peddle and the tires scream out. He sees the Mazda enter the crossroads and hit the Explorer and like two colliding pool balls spin off in opposite directions with debris violently flung into the air.

The truck driver slams on the brakes of the monstrous vehicle to no avail as he plows directly into the side of the police cruiser crushing it beyond recognition and the two go spinning down the road in a heap. Fire has erupted from the ruptured gas tanks and the sparks from the metal that scraped the road. The second officer has arrived and is frantically calling in for an ambulance and fire truck. Shortly more police cars arrive at the scene. The first officer died instantly on impact, a few others in the Explorer were not so lucky. Two severely injured, two killed. The suspect is alive but in critical condition.

Sometime later out in the suburbs another story unfolds. Tommy just took a hit from the joint Billy passed him. Billy is giggling and acting stupid and making faces as he holds his breath from his toke. Sammy had the first hit because he was the one who lit it. They only have one joint between them that they got from an older guy who sells it. Tommy is holding his breath now too making faces back at Billy. Then they all crack up together, acting much like the sixteen-year-olds they are. It's only one skinny joint but they're convinced they all can get stoned off of it. Well at least a little buzz maybe, and they're feeling it already. It doesn't take long to get to the roach and Tommy's the one left with it.

'All right, I get the last hit man…' he says.

'Go for it' says Sammy. They're both giggling some more but not Billy. Tommy looks up at Billy who's pale as a ghost staring off behind him.

'What the hell is with you Billy?' asks Tommy.

'Shit man it's the cops…' says Billy turning and running away.

Tommy and Sammy turn around quickly and see a police car far up the street cruising slowly towards them. Sammy takes off running and in a second or so Tommy flicks the roach away and runs to his bike, jumps on and rides up the street. Having a little buzz amplifies his paranoia as he pedals as hard as he can. He feels compelled to look over his shoulder and he sees the police car turn on its flashing lights and start up the street after him. His heart takes a leap and he's overwhelmed with guilt and he stands on the pedals and gives it everything he's got. He thinks to himself 'Oh man, I can't get in trouble… maybe they'll put me in jail… my dad will kill me… we can't afford a lawyer… got to get the hell out of here!'

The policeman slowly went by the area where the boys were hanging out and thought he smelled marijuana. He looked up the road and could see a red taillight of some sort far up ahead, and put his lights on to follow and stop whoever it was. The vehicle did not stop so he put his siren on.

The sound of the siren makes Tommy's heart skip a beat and his adrenaline flow. 'Oh no he's after me, I can't believe it…' he thinks. Now he's really scared and pedals even harder. He takes a right turn and heads up another street. When he's gone a few blocks he turns to see if the cop is still there. Surely enough the patrol car comes around the corner and up the same road he's on. He turns left onto another road and flies down the street as fast as he can go. The police car is still in pursuit only gaining speed now. He turns out to the highway and crosses the lanes because luckily for him there is no traffic. He looks around behind him and for a few seconds there is no police car. He has a pretty good lead and thinks maybe he can outrun the cop to the turnoff that goes into the woods (and he'll lose him there). There's only one thing he didn't calculate and that was that the police car could go much faster on the highway with no corners to go around. Soon the police car isn't far behind.

The siren sounds really loud now and Tommy's heart is pounding and his mind is racing wildly in fear. Finally he reaches the turnoff to the woods but he's going really fast. He tries to brake the bike a little to make the turn but he hits some gravel in the road. The policeman tries to brake to make the turn also but he's going way too fast. Tommy's bike slips out from under him on the gravel but at the same moment the police car comes sliding into him sideways because the officer is trying to avoid hitting him and had cut the wheel sharply. Tommy is bounced off the side of the car and flies through the air hitting a tree and like a rag doll bounces off down a ravine where he is slammed into some rocks.

The police car screeches off the road and is able to stop just before the tree. The officer cuts the siren off and gets out. He walks down the ravine to the limp body of a teenage boy. He checks Tommy's vital signs then shakes his head a few times, then slowly gets up and returns to the car to radio in what has happened.

TWO

James is leaving work with Bill and starts venting to his buddy:

'You know what really burns me up? How the cops can elevate something as simple as innocent fear or a minor traffic infraction to the level of a life and death situation. Did you read the story about that young kid, a teenager I think, on a bike that was chased by a cop? For some reason the cops found him or the situation suspicious and for some reason the kid got paranoid, maybe a minor infraction of some kind. Anyway, the kid takes off and I don't know if the cop knew it was a bike or not, but whatever, the pursuit is on. After awhile the kid crashes into a tree or down a ravine and is killed. Killed! What the hell was so important to not let it go? Why did this have to be pushed into a dangerous situation? There was no major crime committed except fleeing an officer, which turns out to be a capital crime I guess. They shouldn't be allowed to push a situation to this extreme unless all the facts are in at a felony level. If they're not sure but only "think" or it "appears" to be felonious they shouldn't escalate it immediately but wait and pursue it through other means they have.'

'You're exaggerating!' replies Bill.

'Yeah, you think so? Well try this… Next time you're at a light or stop sign next to a cop, look over at him and turn away quickly, then try to drive away from him or something to get him to follow you. Then take off like a bandit and without committing any crime other than maybe what he might call reckless driving because you took off, you're in a chase. Now your crime is not stopping for an officer. Both these things will cost you your life now if you don't stop and give up but refuse to be taken in. For no other reason than fleeing when a cop thinks you're suspicious you're in a situation of surrender or be killed! Also I heard a story about this guy who had some misdemeanor or minor infraction and the cops were pursuing him as he drove his car. They set up a roadblock ahead of him and when he reached it, he tried to drive around it. The cops opened fire and shot the guy in the head. He wasn't killed because the bullet didn't go into his brain but glanced off. The intention sure as hell was to kill him! And he hadn't committed a capital crime other than fleeing from an officer. They should post that as a capital crime if that's how they treat it.'

'Those are few and far between events, the cops aren't like that as a rule!'

'Yeah, but those events happen, more so than should!' quips James 'and the stinking attitude they have that your all guilty of something and you just haven't been caught yet! Well I think all cops are bad cops, they just haven't been caught yet!'

'There's mistakes and abuses in every walk of life, you think cops are perfect?'

'It's not just cops, it's the whole damn system!'

'With all the people and all the crimes committed I think the system does a good job for what it's dealing with. They have to deal with all the lawyers too!' argues Bill.

'Yeah, that's another whole story!'

'Right! Anyhow did you finish that program for billing?' asks Bill.

'Just before 5:00, I didn't feel like staying late. I'll see how it does over the weekend.'

'What're you doing tonight?'

'Heading up to the mountains' replies James.

'Going up to the mountains again? For the whole weekend?'

'Yeah, I love it up there.'

'O.k., see ya Monday…'

'See ya…'

James gets in his SUV and drives home. For dinner he pops a frozen burrito in the microwave. After dinner he goes to the closet to check some supplies he has stashed there. Its time for another run to the mountains and James is not wealthy but makes enough money to buy survival supplies, some electronic equipment and some contraband materials. He's been regularly going up to the mountains for about a year now. This project he's working on takes time and money and he has to do it by himself. He loads what he needs into the Outback and shuts his place down after double-checking the windows, the stove and all electrical stuff. Now the arduous drive to the mountains. Actually if the traffic's light he'll make it there in a couple of hours. He pops a Craig Chaquico compact disc in the player and heads out. Good luck, the interstate traffic looks light.

Bill goes into the local bar for happy hour. Friday's a good happy hour! After ordering his first twenty-five cent beer he wanders over to the pool table. There are a few quarters down on the table so he knows the next few games are taken. Bill wanders back over to the bar and sees some friends.

'Hey Joey, what's goin' on?'

'Bill, nothin' much, where's your buddy James?'

'Up in the mountains again.'

'What the hell does he do up there all the time?'

'I don't know but he enjoys it, he's always there!'

'You'd think he has a mountain mamma… Wait, I bet that's it! He found a mountain mamma up there and he didn't tell you about her. No wonder he's always up there.'

'He'd tell me man… I know he would. He always tells me about any chicks he meets.'

'Maybe he found a mountain man! Little "Deliverance" thang goin' on…ha ha ha'

72

'Oh cut the crap, you know he's not like that!'

The two order some burgers for dinner and some more beers. It doesn't take much time for them to wolf their food down.

About the time they finish Brenda and Jackie arrive and sachet up to the bar.

'Hey guys...' says Brenda.

'Hey, how you guy's doin'?' replies Bill.

'Friday night party night, you know...'

'Let's get it going... what're you drinkin'?'

Bill orders the girls drinks on him.

'Oh thank you sweetie!' says Jackie taking her drink.

'More where this came from?' asks Brenda.

'If you're a good girl!' says Bill jokingly.

'Forget it!' says Brenda jokingly also.

They all commence to have a good time together playing pool, dancing and telling jokes and gossip.

Its a few hours later and James has reached his destination in the mountains. After navigating many miles of dirt logging roads and back woods paths he stops the Outback. A large lamp-like flashlight is all he needs to get around at night. He goes up to a cave he had found in this mountain a year ago. Since then he has made it into a sort of den with two levels of entrances, a large stone door rolling on ball bearings is the second entrance. Inside he has a lot of electronic equipment, the most important being the generator for power. He turns it on at arrival. Now he has light to see by and turns off the flashlight. He unloads the equipment he

73

brought a little at a time from the SUV. After that chore is done, he sits outside under the stars and moonlit sky showing in between the treetops. He opens a can of cold ginger ale and lights up a nice LaGloria Cubana torpedo cigar. While puffing away heartily he daydreams of the events to come and thinks about how good this cigar is! He wonders if he anticipated enough for his plan. Well, even if most of it went off it still would be cool. After he's done with his cigar he goes to the SUV and brings the cooler back to the cave. He makes sure he's got his eggs and sausage for breakfast on top and the rest of the food for the weekend packed nicely away with juice and milk and a few beers too. Then he closes up and settles down in the cave in his sleeping bag for a good night's sleep. He'll need the rest for tomorrow and Sunday; he's got lots of work to do. This is the finishing check weekend for his project and he has to do it all in two days.

It's Sunday night now, and James has finally returned home. A good weekend, he thinks, he was able to finish all the stuff before going into action tomorrow. He grabs a beer and goes out to the garage. He takes some signs down (that he had previously made) from the shelf. Then he gets some paste like rubber cement and strategically puts it on the back of the signs. Now he sticks the signs on the back and sides of the Subaru. Done! Time to go to bed and rest up; tomorrow ought to be a good one!

THREE

Monday morning at the company and while everyone groggily moves about nursing their coffees someone sees Bill and asks:

'Hey Bill, where's your buddy James? Did he take a day off? Long weekend maybe?'

'Haven't seen him so far. Maybe he'll be late today.'

Bill gets to his cubicle and settles in. Just as he's ready to start the day the manager comes over.

'Have you heard anything from James? He's never late and didn't leave a message about being sick or anything.'

'No I haven't. He went up to the mountains this weekend again, maybe he got stuck somewhere.'

'He's got a cell phone, he'd call someone!'

'Well, I don't know where he is, maybe he'll come in late.'

James is driving up the interstate towards the mountains well within the speed limit. Occasionally some wise guy follows him for a while then passes shouting, "I followed you asshole, I followed you!" Soon a police officer comes up behind him and follows, but not too closely. The officer doesn't quite know what to make of this so he calls in to the station. After identifying himself and giving his location and direction, he starts to inquire:

'I've got an unusual situation here, this guy's driving along with signs on his car that say "I haven't done anything wrong" and "I want to be left alone, do not follow me!" Seems a little unusual to me. The driver is a normal looking male, maybe 30. Should I stop him to see what this is about?'

The station tells him to see if the vehicle fails any safety or standard regulations like the taillights or license plate being covered by the signs. This would be reason enough to stop him. But when the officer replies negative, they ask for the license plate number to run a check on. After a few minutes they report James' name and address and that everything is in order, no problems here. The advice for the officer is to follow him awhile. After following James for about ten minutes, another officer pulls up behind them. He communicates via radio with the first officer who tells him the story, and they both continue to follow. Because they are on the interstate, the second officer falls off and radios a state trooper informing him of the situation. When the state trooper arrives behind the first officer, the first officer drops off and waves bye to the trooper. Now James is being followed by a state trooper but not pulled over. Another trooper going the opposite direction notices the first trooper following an SUV. This prompts him to slow down and make a turn over the grassy median. Now two state troopers are following him. James is very pleased, he's observed this entire sequence happening behind him and feels the plan is now in effect.

Before too long the procession is now at the foothills and continues up to the mountains. James keeps within the speed limit and signals when it's time to turn off on the two lane road leading up to the logging road (which leads up to his little "hideout"). The two troopers follow right behind. They're thinking that even though they have no reason to stop him, when he finally does stop they can at least talk to him about the signs and see if there's any problem. As they all go up the logging road, James increases his speed leaving the troopers struggling with their cars to get up the rough terrain. It doesn't take long for James to get a good lead on them with his all-wheel drive SUV. Soon he is out of their sight.

Finally the two troopers give up. These vehicles can't make it up the logging road and their chances of getting stuck are greatly increasing. They both stop and talk over the situation and decide to radio in for a state police SUV. In about an hour one finally arrives. After explaining everything to the new guy, all three pile in the SUV and head up the logging road. Just a few miles ahead they run into James' Outback that's parked off the road at the base of a meadow. They stop the SUV and get out to look around. They read the signs on the Outback and chuckle to one another. Then they notice a similar sign on a post at the foot of the path heading up the meadow: "I didn't do anything wrong, just go away and leave me alone or I will protect myself from your invasiveness." One asks the others what they're dealing with here. They all conclude at least some kind of a nut.

The officers decide to go up the path and look around. But only after a few steps... BLAM BLAM...shots are fired and they all hit the dirt in one lightning fast reflex motion. They wait a few minutes... its quiet, no more shots. Now they feel it's safe to get up. As they start one of them moans and says, "Oh shit, my ankle". He had jerked his leg violently because his foot was unbalanced on a rock as he dropped to the ground from the shots. He doesn't know if it's broken but he can't walk on it, way too much pain. The others decide they have to get him back to town and with only one vehicle they decide that they all have to leave. When they get to their cars, they leave one there as one of them drives the other car and the injured one goes back with the SUV.

After they arrive at the trooper station, arrangements are made for the injured one to have x-rays. They find him a pair of crutches to help him walk. As they're sitting in the front reception area the Chief comes out to talk with them. They fill him in on the whole story and he throws his head back and exclaims:

'What the hell do we have here, a goddamn "Unabomber" or something?'

'I don't think so Chief, his report is clean and he looks real normal. Maybe he lost his girl or something and this is his way of

78

getting attention. People are strange these days' says one of the troopers.

'Well he fired shots at you, that's pretty serious.'

The other trooper joins in:

'We didn't see him fire the shots, just saw his car there. Someone else could have fired them.'

'Yeah but the sign did say he would "protect' himself"' retorts the Chief. 'Well I'm going up there tomorrow with the County Sheriff and see what's going on. Let's get Chuck to the hospital for x-rays.'

The Chief, one of the troopers and Chuck (the hurt one) pile into the Chiefs SUV and head out to the hospital. The other covers for the Chief at the station. After the x-rays, Chuck receives good news, no broken bones! However he still has to mend from a severe sprained ankle.

It's morning, a beautiful morning at that with wisps of fog appearing stuck to trees and shrubs like cotton candy while the sun sheds bright yellow rays on the forest that appear blue-gray through the fog patches. The Chief and County Sheriff are driving up to the last reported spot where the troopers were shot at. The trooper who left his car is with them to retrieve it and drive it back. They turn off the interstate onto the two-lane road soon becoming a dirt road and now a logging trail. After following the trail for a while they come upon the trooper's car and let him out. Then they drive farther up to James' car still parked where it was the day before. The two get out of their SUV and read the signs on the car.

'You know Chief, when someone puts signs like these on a car they want you to follow them' says George the County Sheriff.

'I guess. Let's see what's going on.'

'There's another sign over here by the path, guess that's where the boys got shot at.'

'O.K. We've got to go up there too, keep it low and cool and let's keep our eyes open.'

They make it about fifty feet up the path then shots ring out and they both drop.

'You all right?' asks the Chief.

'Yeah, how about you?'

'O.K.'

They both lay low for a few minutes looking around.

'Either he's a lousy shot or he doesn't want to hit us Chief' says George.

'No, it's more than that... Did you hear anything in the trees behind us?'

'No'

'Well don't you think those bullets should have ripped through them making some noise?'

'Yeah, I guess so.'

'He's shooting blanks!'

'You sure?'

'Sure enough to do this!' and the Chief stands up again. He walks forward a little... then more shots... but he doesn't drop.

'What the hell are you doing?' exclaims George.

'I'm not hit. They're blanks I told you.'

George gets up warily and starts to move forward... BLAM, BLAM, BLAM... more shots, but George isn't hit either.

'Well I'll be damned, ha ha, that's not a good feeling hearing those shots and standing up in front of them!'

'Did you see anything or anyone?' asks the Chief.

'No, but the shots came from that clump of bushes ahead, I saw the flash and smoke that time.'

They both make their way up to the bushes slowly. As they approach they can make out something in them. With weapons drawn they move right up to it.

'What is it?' asks George.

'Looks like some automated contraption' answers the Chief as he tears away some of the brush.

'That's what it is, I can see the barrel holes in it where the shots came out and that thing on top is probably a detection unit of some kind that triggers it to fire.'

The Chief waves a stick across the front, but nothing.

'Must be out of ammo' he says then stands in front of it.

'Yep, it's out.'

'You're a hell of a daredevil Chief!' exclaims George 'it's a wonder you're still alive.'

'I only do this stuff when I'm sure, I don't take uncalculated risks.'

'Well, what now?'

'Let's go on up some more, there's another sign up there.'

The two go up the path farther until they can read the next sign. "I didn't do anything wrong, leave me alone" it reads "do not come any farther, there are land mines ahead if you do. If you don't believe me, throw a rock on the red circled area."

'What the hell… this is getting serious, landmines!' says the Chief.

'Could be bluffing…'

'Where's the red circle?'

'Right up there, can you throw that far with a good sized rock?' asks George.

'Sure… and here's a good-sized rock. Why don't you stand back just in case…'

The Chief takes aim and heaves the rock at the red-circled area. Nothing… he missed!

'Ha ha ha ha… you missed it!'

'O.K. George, you take a crack at it.'

George finds a rock, takes aim and tosses it right on target — WHAM — and the two of them hit the dirt.

'Goddamn… you all right?' asks the Chief.

'Yeah, just some dirt on me.'

'I guess he wasn't kidding, and that's no blank!'

'This is more serious than I thought now. We'd better get the Guard in on this. I'm not risking going any farther and you're not either.'

'O.K. George, I hear you, I'm not going out there...'

The two get back to their vehicle and drive down the mountain swiftly. When they get to the trooper station, George calls the local National Guard and explains the situation. After the proper authorities are notified and briefed, they wait for orders.

FOUR

Back in town Bill wonders what happened to James. It's been a couple of days now and no one has heard anything. He decides to go on over to James' place and check it out. He has a key James left with him for emergencies. He goes in and checks the place out thoroughly but nothing seems out of place or suspicious. It's just like it always is when James goes to the mountains. Still, something's not right. He decides to call the police. The local cops haven't heard anything and suggest he try the state troopers, they would know about what's going on in the mountains. Apparently the local cops who saw the car with the signs turned it over to the troopers and forgot about it.

After the usual red tape and explanation of who he is (and that James is his best buddy but hasn't been around for days) the trooper's office informs him that his friend may be in some sort of trouble. They ask Bill to come on in to talk with them. So he heads down to the trooper station.

'So this guy James is your best buddy?' asks the Chief.

'Yes sir, he is.'

'Has he been acting strange lately?'

'No, just goes up to the mountains by himself a lot.'

'What's he do up there?'

'Don't know for sure... maybe fish and hunt or just be alone for a while. Some guys think he's met a mountain mamma up there and goes to see her, but I know he didn't.'

'Has he been complaining or blowing off steam about anything?'

'No... not that I can think of... I mean the guy's always cynical of idiots, he's pretty bright and a good computer programmer. The normal dumbing down of the masses always bothers him. Sometimes he goes on about stuff like that. But not a rant, you know...'

'Does he have a girl he might be breaking up with?'

'Not now, hasn't had a girlfriend for about a year. How about letting me know what's going on here.'

'Nothing to worry about yet... your buddy here put some signs on his car like "I didn't do anything wrong, don't follow me!" and of course that made us a little suspicious. A couple of troopers followed him up to a place in the mountains where he seems to be maybe hiding out or something. A few shots were fired but when I went up they turned out to be blanks. When the Sheriff and I investigated further, we found a land mine and triggered it. It blew... so now there's a real danger here. The

National Guard was called in and they're doing a mine sweep of the meadow up there. This could be your buddy doing this.'

'I don't think so. Not land mines anyhow! James is a little strange but not this crazy…'

'His car is still up there so it sure looks like it's him. Why don't you come with me up there and maybe we can try and talk with him. I'll call the guard and get permission to come up.'

So the Chief and Bill are on their way to the mountains. After some small talk and lots of country music they arrive at their destination. The Guard cordoned off the area, so the Chief has to present his permission to be there. He explains whom Bill is and the two are allowed to proceed. At the meadow the Major confronts them.

'Howdy Chief, haven't seen you for a good while…'

'Major, how've you been?'

'Fine, fine, so who do we have here?'

'He's the best buddy of the guy who owns the Outback, his name is Bill.'

'Howdy Bill, looks like your buddy might have a problem of some sort.'

'Yes sir, it appears that way' says Bill shaking his head while reading the signs on the Subaru.

'Not much so far Chief… the one mine that blew seems like the only active thing out there. We found four other buried disks… they were all Frisbees! Maybe it's a joke but we have to take the whole thing seriously. What do you think Bill?'

'Oh no, now I remember… He went on one day about the cops chasing people even if there was no crime committed and how some got killed for just running from them and how unfair that is. He's doing this to prove it. That's why the signs "I didn't do anything wrong".'

'Well he's done a few things wrong now son' says the Major.

'If in fact it is him' says the Chief 'we haven't made contact yet to be sure.'

'It's him…' says Bill 'you notice he didn't really try to hurt anyone. The shots were blanks, there are no more landmines and he knew you'd blow the one he pointed out with the sign. Listen, why can't we just all go home and leave him alone, that would end his trying to prove you won't.'

'Can't do that son' says the Major 'he's gone too far with it; we have to have some closure now. We all have people to answer to you know.'

'I hope you're not planning to hurt him in any way.'

'No we're not, as long as he cooperates with us he's in no danger. You can help us here you know kind of talk him into cooperating huh?'

'Have you contacted him?'

'Not yet' says the Major 'but we will.'

The Major now gives some commands to his men to proceed farther up the meadow and investigate. The men move forward and encounter no shots or mines or other problems. A path seems to lead up to a steep hillside dead end. When they get closer they see a small cave with a crude wooden door closing the entrance. On the door is written "Go away and leave me alone, why are you intruding upon me? I didn't do anything wrong!"

'This must be the place!' says one of the guardsmen.

Another one begins to pound on the door 'Anyone in there?' he yells. There is no response. He pounds some more yet harder and yells louder 'Hey, anyone home… anyone in there?' Still there is no response. By this time the Chief the Major and Bill arrive at the cave.

'Bill, why don't you give it a try, see if your buddy will respond to your voice?' says the Major.

'O.k.' So Bill pauses a moment then yells as loud as he can 'James, you in there? Hey James it's me Bill, What's going on buddy?' But there's no response.

'O.k. you men, let's see if we can pry it open. Get some shovels or crowbars and axes and bust this thing off' commands the Major.

A few men go back to the road and retrieve the equipment from their Humvees. When they return they begin to pry at the door with crowbars in any crevice they can. It's not working, they're just busting off wood chips, and the door is very thick. The shovels are no good either because the door is on rock.

'Damn, this thing's pretty stubborn. Well instead of breaking our backs on it, someone go down and drive a Humvee with a winch on it up here. We'll pull the damn thing off' orders the Major.

After a few minutes they hear the Humvee's engine start up, then the crunch of twigs and leaves and rocks flying out from under the tires as it makes its way up the meadow. They all turn around to watch it coming up when suddenly the wheels spin wildly and the whole thing drops into the ground in a crash of dirt and rocks and wood. A large cloud of dust and debris is thrown up into the air.

'What the hell…' shouts the Chief.

'Jesus Christ!' the Major starts in 'you men get down there and see what happened and help that soldier out!'

The men have gotten down to the wreck before the Chief, Major and Bill. Some of them are down in the ground helping the driver get out. When the Major arrives at the scene one of the men says:

'It's a ravine sir, must have been covered up with logs and dirt and leaves to look natural. It was a trap, when the Humvee passed over the weight was too much and it gave way.'

'Is the driver all right?'

'I'm fine sir' says the driver.

'Bring up another one and we'll pull her out' says the Major.

'I suspect our boy did this too' says the Chief 'he knew we'd try to get some heavy equipment up here, pretty clever boy.'

'Still, he's not really trying to harm anyone' says Bill.

It takes awhile to get the Humvee out, pulling it up with it's own winch and the other Humvee. But they do get it out and being the tough machine it is, it starts right up and is ready to go.

Just a few dents and scratches here and there. The Major gives the command to set camp, it is getting late and will be dark soon. He sends a man back to headquarters for a drill, some stumping powder sticks, and electronic detonator caps to bring up tomorrow. The plan now is to blow the door off. They'll try to contact James verbally and warn him.

FIVE

Soon some campfires are set and everyone settles down in groups for some chow. It looks like a Boy Scout camping trip now. It feels that way too. It's a beautiful night to be out in the woods camping.

The men are talking and sharing jokes and playing games. Tonight they sleep in shifts so there's always one group awake throughout the night.

'What a beautiful night' the Major says to the Chief.

'Yeah, too bad we're up here on business' he responds 'I don't know what it is with these crazy kids these days... damn I sound like my father did years ago. Even so, they didn't quite do the things they do today! Don't they know the consequences of taking actions like they do?'

'Don't seem to care' says the Major 'they get something in their head and go right off to do it... don't think much about it or what could happen to them if it doesn't go their way.'

'I don't know… can't figure them out. Might as well just try to keep up with them only we're filling up all the damn jails! And sometimes the kids are good kids like this James is. Bill, what makes you guys do these things?'

'Hell, I don't know, I don't do this stuff and certainly nothing worse than this. And like I said before, James is just trying to make a point. He isn't into breaking the law or being a criminal or anything like it. He's just playing a game. I think he's doing it so he doesn't drive himself nuts about how he feels about cop chases where people get killed for no reason.'

'I'd say he already drove himself nuts by all this he's doing…' chuckles the Chief 'not very normal behavior to me!'

'Just don't be too tough on him o.k? You can see he's not trying to hurt anyone.'

'Being tough on him is going to be in the hands of the court son, we can't do much about that. But believe me I will do what I can to help the boy.'

'Thanks Chief… guess he's going to need some help.'

So the three go on making some more small talk and slowly become drowsy enough to go off to bed. The night is dark and cool and quieting down with the men now rapidly falling off to sleep. Soon all are sleeping except for a small group left on watch. A few hours pass peacefully past midnight as the breeze whispers through the trees and the muffled snores of some of the men rhythmically blend with the sounds of crickets and chirping frogs. No one notices the grass moving a little and then all around. It is moving, and even more so each minute, and all over the camp. Within minutes the grass in the whole camp looks like it's rippling with little waves. There's also some movement under some of the sleeping bags and blankets. One soldier rolls over under his blanket and feels a tickling sensation on his face that he immediately swipes at and ignores. In another few seconds he feels it again, but this time with a little cold wet spot. As he opens his eyes two tiny eyes are staring back.

'What the hell' he shouts jumping up swinging his arms at anything. This alarms a few others who wake up and some are shouting also feeling little feet scattering over their bodies.

'What the hell is this?' many are asking.

'It's rats... rats are all over...' is the reply.

A few of the men grab their pistols and start shooting at the rats. This wakes everyone up quickly. The major takes command.

'Hold your fire damn it hold your fire! It's just some damn rats, they're more afraid of you!'

The rats are scurrying everywhere as the men stomp at them and chase them around and swing at them with whatever they can get their hands on. Soon order is restored to the camp and the rats have fled.

'Where the hell did these things come from?' asks the Chief.

'Well rats are always in the woods somewhere but it's unusual that they come out like this. Maybe the food brought them in but not all at once in such numbers. I bet our friend has something to do with this. He probably had them all cooped up somewhere then let them loose while we were sleeping' explains the Major. Then he addresses the men.

'O.k. it's over now, get your butts back to sleep 'cause I want everyone fresh in the morning.'

The men gladly obey and return to their sleeping places chuckling a little at their own reactions to this little episode.

SIX

It's morning and the men are all up getting coffee and breakfast from the re-lit campfires. The whole camp smells like fresh coffee. The men who went for the stumping sticks have returned. The Major greets the Chief and Bill:

'Morning guys, how'd you sleep out here in the woods? When's the last time you camped out? Great ain't it?'

'You bet, except for the rats' says the Chief 'can't beat a morning like this.'

'Thanks for the tent and sleeping bags Major' says Bill.

'Oh no problem son, we spend a lot of time outdoors so we're equipped! Come on over to my camp and get some breakfast.'

'Man that coffee smells good' says Bill eyeing the pot.

'Well go get you some boy. And get some eggs and pancakes and sausages' exclaims the Major.

'Wow, you guys really eat good out here.'

'Well we're so close to home we can get all this stuff easy, so we do it up!'

After breakfast they go over to the staging area and check out the supplies. There's a box of stumping powder sticks and a box of blasting caps and a drill with large bits and an auger bit.

'This ought to do the trick on that door, we'll drill a hole with the auger bit and slip in a stick of powder, only enough to blow the door' explains the Major. So they're off up the meadow with some of the men carrying the supplies and soon stop and set everything at the mouth of the cave. One man begins drilling a hole at the bottom of the door. The hole is the right size to slip a stick of the powder into. The stick has a blasting cap with wires connected for firing. The Major comes over with a bullhorn and starts talking to Bill.

'O.k. son, I want you to take this bullhorn and explain to your friend what we're doing and what's going to happen. And tell him to take cover!' Bill nods and takes the bullhorn pointing it at the cave. He presses the switch and starts:

'James, it's Bill, if you can hear me listen carefully. They're going to blast your door out with some dynamite. So get yourself under cover now! I'm not kidding James… get yourself protected!'

There's no response from the cave. They hook up the wires to the hand generator and wait.

Still there is no response from the cave. The Major signals everyone to move back, far back. When they're all out of danger he signals the man holding the generator. With one twist, the spark is sent to the dynamite and the door shatters in pieces at the blast. They all return to the cave to find another obstacle not far behind where the door was. It's a large rock wedged in the cave blocking any passage. Something is chiseled in the rock so they come closer to read it. It's pretty messed up with debris, so the Major wipes it with his hands.

'What's it say? Is that "One"? Is it "One good…" is that "boom", is that what it says? "One good boom deserves another"?'

'That's what it says Major' replies the Chief.

'I don't like it, maybe we should…' the Major can't finish… BOOM… the forest echoes the sound all around. All the men turn around to see smoke and debris and broken trees all around their vehicles back at the bottom of the meadow. The Major signals to get down there thinking James is there and has set off this explosion. When they get there they can see the busted trees. Someone had hid dynamite in the trees around the bottom of the meadow and set it off. They notice the cap wires too and follow them to where they go beneath the ground. They pull them up as they go and finally are back at the cave where they go under the rock into it.

'He blew it from inside the cave! He knows what we're doing out here. Look for more wires under the dirt' orders the Major.

They find another wire covered by dirt leading into the cave. When they pull it up it leads back to some trees.

97

'Look up in those trees' says the Major 'you'll probably find a surveillance camera!'

Sure enough up in one tree facing the mouth of the cave is a camera. One of the men climbs up and retrieves it.

Back down the hill a truck approaches and parks where the other vehicles are. Two men get out and show identification to the guards. The Major remarks to the Chief:

'Oh well, here come the big boys. I knew they'd get wind of this sooner or later.'

'What? The FBI'

'You guessed it, get ready to take orders!' he says to the Chief, and now in a loud voice 'Everyone down the hill and fall in at the staging area now!'

The men drop what they're doing and go down to the staging area as the Major, Bill and the Chief follow. When they get there the Major goes up to the two men.

'Good day gentlemen, I'm the Major in command here at your service.'

One of them responds: 'this is agent Thompson and I'm agent Jorgsen; Federal Bureau of Investigation.'

'This is the local Chief of the state police, and this is Bill. Bill is the suspect's best friend, anything you need to know just ask.'

'Yes we know about Bill.' Then the other agent starts talking. 'James is a good man; he has no record or past history of instability. He comes from a good family. He keeps good well-adjusted friends like Bill here. He keeps steady employment and he's a good worker. He doesn't do drugs and seldom gets drunk. He's well educated and fits in with society. What makes him do this?'

'Bill thinks he's just trying to prove a point' says the Major 'he complained to Bill about cop chases where someone gets killed just for running from them even though no crime was proven committed.'

'I think he's trying to show that even though he didn't do anything he became suspicious to the police and they'd escalate the situation to this instead of leaving it be at it's inception' interjects Bill.

'Well we'll leave all that to the shrinks for later, right now we need to get him in custody' says Thompson. Just then he looks back down the trail and his face sours. 'Oh shit, here comes the freak show!'

A local TV station truck is lumbering up the trail towards them and right behind is another from a major station. The Guard stops them at the staging area. The Major is called over to negotiate.

'We have a right to be here Major' says one of the TV Crew 'we want full access.'

'No one's stopping you, you just have to comply with our movements because there has been danger demonstrated here. Just stay back and obey our commands if we need you to get out of harm's way.'

The crews unpack all their paraphernalia and begin setting up. One crew is on this side and the other on that side. There are lights and cameras, microphones and wires everywhere. The Guardsmen are cleaning up the debris on everything from the blasted trees. Soon one crew starts to record.

'We're in the mountains just a few miles outside of Melville at a site where what seems to be some kind of explosion took place. There are trees split apart everywhere. The National Guard is here also and we have the Major here to explain. Major, can you explain what's happened here?'

'Yes I can. We have a situation here where a man after acting suspiciously drove to this site and barricaded himself into a cave. Troopers have been shot at but it turns out the shots were blanks. A land mine was detonated in this field so the National Guard was called in to sweep the meadow for other mines.

We're glad to report no other mines were found. The suspect detonated some dynamite strapped to trees down here. We think this was in response to our blasting his outer wooden door off of the cave. There is another stone blocking the entrance to the cave. We haven't made verbal contact with the suspect yet but we keep trying. We're going to have to remove the stone to apprehend the suspect.'

'We understand the suspect's name is James and he is a local computer programmer.'

'I can't say at this point. Like I said we haven't made contact with the suspect at this time.'

'Why is he doing this? What crime did he commit.'

'You'll have to talk to the Chief about that.'

The Chief is called and he reluctantly meanders over to the camera.

'Chief, can you tell us what crime has been committed here and why the suspect was chased up here to this cave.'

'First of all, the suspect was not "chased" up here. He drove up on his own accord. He was driving with signs on his car that seemed a little strange to our troopers, so they followed him to see what it was about. There was no crime committed. When they got to this meadow they were shot at. Even though the bullets were blanks, this now became a fairly serious situation. The Major and myself detonated a land mine so we called the Guard to come in and sweep for others. No others were found. At this point it became imperative that we apprehend the suspect.'

Meanwhile the crew has pulled Bill over for his own interview. The camera switches to Bill and the questions start.

'There you have it. We now have the suspect's best friend here...'

'Is that all?' asks the Chief. 'For now' is the reply.

'So Bill, we understand James is your best friend.'

'Yes he is.'

'Have any idea why he's doing this?'

'Well, he kind of has this pet peeve about police chasing innocent or at least not clearly guilty persons and putting them in a life and death situation only because they're fleeing. Many of

101

these pursuits end in death for somebody… and what for? Justice? Of what? A crime wasn't proven! So I think this is his way of bringing attention to it. He hasn't done anything wrong yet here he is being flushed out by police for what? Because he had some funny signs on his car and they thought he was suspicious of something I guess.'

'But what about the shots and land mines? This seems pretty serious and certainly wrong!'

'Those are the results of the police intruding up here after they already started following him when he didn't do anything wrong.'

'Certainly many questions for the legal community. Right now though do you think he'll come out?'

'I hope so, I don't want to see him get hurt.'

'We'll be talking some more later with the players in this bizarre game in the woods, now back to the studio.'

SEVEN

The Major is standing before the stone at the cave entrance thinking out loud.

'What do we do with this? Damn thing's too big to move. Picks won't break it up anytime soon. We've already blasted. Too dangerous to blast rock, someone will get killed! How about a jackhammer, we got a jackhammer somewhere?'

'We've got one back at the station sir with a mobile generator' says a Guardsman.

'All right soldier, you're responsible for getting it and as soon as you can.'

With that the soldier heads down the hill and takes a couple of others with him in a Humvee and goes back to the Guard station. The Major orders everyone to take a break and get some chow. In a couple of hours the soldiers return with a generator and jackhammer. After hooking everything up they tell the Major they're ready. He tells them to start on the rock at the top and work down. After a few minutes of severe vibration and chunks of rock flying, what seems to be the cave ceiling collapses on and all over the men and equipment.

'Oh man… what the hell… it's manure! Aah that stinks awful' exclaims one of the men. It's fallen on four men and they walk back out to the Major. 'Minor problem sir' says one of them.

'Yes we can smell that' says the Major jokingly 'you men go down and find some creek and wash up. Let's get someone in here and clean it up.'

The chief and Bill are laughing out loud. The Major says to them 'your boy has a sense of humor! What's next?'

The cameras are picking up the men leaving the cave drenched in manure while the reporters make their quips and jokes. The mess at the rock door is cleaned up enough to continue work on it. The jackhammers are started up again and drilling continues. The rock is breaking slowly in small chunks from the jackhammers. The Chief is watching intently when he notices something.

'Wait a minute' he shouts 'stop drilling, whoa, whoa…'

'What is it Chief?' asks the Major after the jackhammers stop.

'Look at the right side, see that indentation in the crease there? You can fit your hands behind it, looks like it was made for that.'

'Yeah could be' says the Major 'one of you men try pulling that rock from that spot.'

One of the Guardsmen reaches around the indentation with both hands and pulls.

'It's coming sir, I feel movement...' He keeps pulling and slowly the rock rumbles back opening from that side. 'Huh... damn thing must be on a roller or ball bearings or something!'

'Good work soldier' says the Major.

When the rock door is pulled all the way back, it reveals another wooden door and another message written across it: "Why can't you leave me alone?"

'How many damn doors are we going to have to go through?' asks the Major out loud 'well, at least this one's wood again!'

'We've got a metal handle on this one sir' says a soldier 'maybe we can just pull it open.'

The soldier grabs the handle and pulls hard. The door doesn't move but the handle slides right out with a rectangular box attached with no top. He holds it for a second then screams out loud and drops it and runs back. As soon as it hits the ground a massive swarm of bees emerges and spreads all over the cave site in seconds. Everyone is running this way and that to get out of their way, swatting the air and themselves as they go. The Major and the Chief and Bill run down to the staging area. The men are yelling from the stings and smacking the bees on them. It seems as if everyone has been stung at least once. Even the cameramen have stopped filming to get out of there away from the bees.

'You're boy's starting to piss me off! This one wasn't so funny!' exclaims the Major.

'He just wants you to leave him alone…' says Bill.

'Oh we'll leave him alone all right! In a goddamn cell for a long while!' retorts the Major.

'I still think it's pretty damn funny!' says the Chief and starts cracking up 'did you see the face on that soldier when he knew what it was? Ha, ha, ha, ha… did you see everyone scramble like hell! Ha, ha, ha, ha… oh man it was funny all right. I haven't seen you move your ass like that in a long time! Ha, ha, ha, ha…'

'Yeah, well I hope you got stung right on your fat ass!' says the Major laughingly 'damn, bees… haven't been stung in years. Well let's get that box out of there and let these bees move on so we can get that door open.'

The men clear the box out, the bees have flown away except for a few lingerers but they're not stinging anyone. Everyone is back at the door inspecting it and thinking of a way to open it when a voice is heard behind the door in the cave. 'Don't open the door!'

'Some one's in there Major!' shouts a soldier.

'O.k. back away and let me in there.' The Major goes up to the door and says in a loud voice 'Is that you James?'

'Yes, it's me.'

'Why don't you come on out now and talk about all this?'

'Don't open the door.'

'We're not opening any door, just come out now and we can talk.'

'The door's triggered to an explosive, if you open it, it will blow the whole cave!'

'Whoa, hold on now son, no need to get excited.'

'I'm not excited. You should have left me alone. Leave me alone now!'

'You know after all that's happened here we can't do that now.'

'You couldn't do it before, when you should have.'

'James, this is Bill… what's up man? You know you can come out, these guys aren't going to be hard on you!'

'I know it's you Bill! You think I can't recognize your voice, you don't have to tell me who it is!'

'Sorry man… all this stuff has me acting like these guys!'

'Your not a part of this Bill, you ought to go home.'

'Well not now, I want to see you o.k. You know?'

'I am o.k. Especially if I'm just left alone!'

'Listen James' says the Major 'you think about it for a while, we're going down the hill to think about it too. You come on out if you decide, you'll be all right.'

The Major orders everyone back to the staging area.

'Think your pal will come out Bill?' asks the Major.

'Nope!'

'That's what I was afraid of…'

'Sooner or later we'll get into that cave… what do you think he'll do then?' asks the Chief.

'I don't know… I don't think he'll get violent though; he's not like that. I bet he'll just give up once you get in.'

'I hope so' says the Major 'we don't want to get mean and have anybody hurt, and I mean my men also. He'd better not have a gun on him when we get in.'

'I seriously doubt he will' says Bill.

'How much time do we give him to think Chief?' asks the Major.

'Half hour's good… longer only gives him more time to think up some other crazy stuff, shorter and he's still nervous and can't get it together.'

'O.k. We'll go back up in half an hour' says the Major to all present.

It's a long half-hour even though it's nice being out in the woods. This time everyone's quiet. The sounds of birds and the breeze rustling through the trees are all that's heard for a while. Even the news crews are quiet. Finally the time is up. They all return to the cave.

'Have you thought about coming out James?' says the Major.

After a pause there comes a response from inside the cave:

'I'm not coming out. Leave me alone. I didn't hurt anyone and I did no wrong. All this is a result of you following me. You're treating me like it's my fault when all the reactions are your fault for pursuing me here. Why can't you go and leave me alone?'

'You know son we can probably drop all this and work with you to clear it up if you'll just come out' responds the Major.

'Bullshit... you know I'll need a good lawyer!'

'O.k. James no one's trying to say nothing's going to happen. But if you come out it can be worked out and you'll probably come out all right. This is probably not jail sort of stuff, you did no wrong at the start and I don't believe you meant to harm anyone. Everyone here will vouch for that and I think the Chief will support you too.'

'Yes I will' says the Chief 'I don't see any major violations here that cannot be explained or any criminal behavior. As far as I'm concerned it's just a misunderstanding of what you're trying to tell us. And if you come out on your own it's even better for you getting through this.'

'I just want to be left alone! If you can get me through this in court, why can't you just get me through it now and leave!'

The Chief shakes his head and answers 'because we're in the field in the action, not in a court where everything can be brought to light. We don't have all the answers for everybody out here so we have to follow procedure. We're just trying to get you your day in court to make your case.'

'I've already made my case! Once you've swallowed the bait of suspicion the machinery was set in motion, and now you won't leave me alone until I'm apprehended or killed.'

'Now hold on son' blurts the Major 'you're taking this to extremes, no one's getting killed!'

'If you open this door it's going to blow this cave to hell, and I don't think there will be much left of me and anyone out there too close!'

'We're not opening the door, we're going to talk some more out here for awhile' says the Major.

The Chief is pacing back and forth, the Major is pacing back and forth, and Bill... old Bill is just sitting there with his head resting on both hands with a forlorn look on his face.

'What can we do?' asks the Major.

'Beats me!' says the Chief.

'Can't we just leave him alone like he wants? Isn't there some way to go home and forget it?' says Bill.

The Major starts in: 'don't be naïve boy; we have to answer to everyone now, even the public thanks to the news crews. Do you think all those people and our bosses will just forget about it? They all probably want to know more about it now rather than forget it. And do you think they're going to leave him alone? Fat chance! We have to resolve this somehow.'

EIGHT

The two federal agents come into the cave opening while everyone is still thinking about the situation.

'Do we have anything happening yet? Is he coming out?'

'No... he's threatened to blow the cave up if we try to open the door, it's rigged to explosives' answers the Major.

'Well we can't have him do that, he'll kill himself' responds Jorgsen.

'Why don't we call in for a shrink to talk him out' says Thompson. They all seem to agree that this is the best strategy for now; they can't take the chance that he really will blow the cave and kill himself.

Thompson pulls out a cell phone and starts dialing while walking out of the cave entrance. A voice comes from behind the door again.

'Don't bother trying to get someone up here to talk me out, I'm not coming out... go away and leave me alone!'

'James this is agent Jorgsen of the FBI, this situation is under our control. You can trust us to safely bring you out and give you the chance to explain your side of all this to people who will listen and respond to your ideas. We are not interested in prosecution, just understanding. We have whole departments dedicated to understanding the individual and why he does what he does. They are very supportive of individuals like you in a non-criminal situation who need to be heard. All we ask is a chance and that you come out on your own.'

'Agent Jorgsen, this is James of the citizens of America; the situation is under my control. You can trust me not to come out. I've already explained myself. I am not interested in shaming you but want you to just get the hell out of here. All I ask is a chance and that you'll leave on your own and not have me blow anyone up.'

'We're way past leaving you alone James you know that. Now make it easy on yourself and do things our way and you'll be all right.'

'You're not leaving?'

'We're not leaving…'

'You've got thirty seconds to find shelter from the blast…'

A repetitive beep starts going like when a truck backs up, agent Jorgsen shouts loudly to all that are there:

'Let's get the hell out of here!'

Bill shouts out also: 'James don't do this man this is crazy… cut the crap now, this isn't funny!'

'Get the hell down the hill now!' orders Jorgsen to Bill.

They all go running down the slope as fast as they can to take cover behind the Humvees and tree stumps at the staging area. There are cameramen running backwards trying to catch all the action. There's only about five seconds left, it's dead silent except for the incessant beeping, the time seems to have slowed down, as each second seems like a minute... then BOOM; the forest is reverberating with the sound for miles. Debris flies everywhere, tree branches, dust and dirt, stones, rocks and smoke. Everyone is on the ground protecting himself. The dust takes a few minutes to settle and the men begin to stir. Each one gets up slowly to look at the cave. The hill it was on is flat now. Where the cave was is a pile of rocks and dirt filling an indentation in the ground. The Major is the first to speak:

'Damn crazy cracker! What in the hell did he do it for?'

'Oh man' says Bill 'I didn't think he'd really blow the cave, not really... oh James man, you really went way out of it this time!'

'All right' says Jorgsen 'let's try and find some remains or something up there.'

The cameras are back at the site greedily trying to get anything, especially a body in their view.

'I can't watch this, just can't... I don't believe this... this is too much!' says Bill and walks away down the trail shaking his head. He stops at James' Subaru and sits in putting both hands up on top of the steering wheel and rests his head on them. He wants

113

to cry for James but he's in too much shock. Everything is surreal around him and he can't believe James killed himself.

All they can find at the site is some wood and Styrofoam pieces and some wires and pieces of equipment, some food residue and water and some burnt pieces of a sleeping bag. After an hour or so of rummaging the agents call everyone down to the staging area. Jorgsen does the talking:

'All right everyone, show's over. We're calling in a forensic team to glean for the body parts. You can all go home now it's over. We'll issue a report after we see what we find, at this point we can't determine if there is a body or not.'

So all the teams start packing up mumbling this and that about the whole situation and shaking their heads as they talk. No one feels like they've done justice but rather took part in a tragedy. The news teams are running with the story that James, a confused distraught young man upset by fatal police chases, blew himself up in the cave.

Bill returns home with the Chief, both are very silent all the way. This time the radio is not playing. When they get back to Bill's place, the Chief places his hand on Bill's shoulder in a fatherly manner and says:

'I'm sorry for your pal son, it doesn't look good but we haven't found any remains yet. Maybe he's alive still somewhere out there. I'll call you when I get a full report.'

'Thanks Chief... see you later.'

It only takes about a week until the Chief calls. The news is good in kind of a way. A body was not found at the cave. Not even body parts or remains of any kind. A mangled generator and a small metal bent out of shape speaker frame were found. The consensus is that James was not in the cave and spoke to them on the speaker that was probably inside. He's still considered alive and a fugitive from the law.

This is good news for Bill, he thinks to himself 'James you old son of a bitch, I knew you wouldn't kill yourself!' and jumps into his car to go up to the cave and look around. When he gets there, the area has been cleared and nothing remains from the police and the Guard. James' car is no longer there, probably impounded. He walks around where the cave was, and then yells out:

'James you turkey, where the hell are you?'

There's no response, just birds and the sound of the breeze. He walks farther out by the woods looking around like he may see James out here. As he's wandering something brushes across his shoulder. He swipes it out of the way as if it were a thin vine or something. Then he stops, 'Wait a minute' he thinks 'there are no vines up here'. He turns around and looks up at the 'vine'. It's a wire hanging down from a tree. He grabs it and pulls slightly to see where it comes from. It seems to go high up into the tree until he can't see anymore because of all the branches. Now his curiosity is sparked. He goes about climbing into the tree and starts upward. It's a little tough getting through the branches, but he gets up higher above them and he sees a little roughly made tree house. He notices the wire goes up to it also, so he climbs on until he reaches it. A couple of throw pillows are wedged into some branches and there's a black box with some switches on it and a small microphone perched up above it. He can see where the cave was clearly from here. He thinks 'this is where James must have been watching us and talking to us in the microphone and setting things off with the switch box. The wire was probably cut and hidden after James left but came loose and dangled down the tree'. Then he thought James might have left it this way for him to find! Anyhow, he now knows his buddy is alive and probably well... and maybe in Mexico by now! He thinks to himself 'Well James, this is our little secret now, no one will ever know from me buddy!' He pulls the wire up and wraps it around a branch then climbs down. From the bottom, you can't see anything up in the tree because the branches hide it and it's pretty high up. Bill is confident no one will see anything, and the chances of someone climbing up for no reason are slim to none.

Bill drives home chuckling to himself all the way thinking of this whole ordeal and what James has pulled off. It's a beautiful day in the mountains, the sun streaming in and the breeze blowing through the windows, the air is fresh and the music coming from his stereo soothing and this smile will not leave his face.

NINE

The weekend is here at last. Bill decides to call his girlfriend Brenda and ask her to go to the mountains with him for the weekend. There are cabins for rent by the ranger station high up in the mountains far away from the stress and bustle of the towns. It's very rustic up there and not many people know of this area because they all go to the more commercial cabins by the main road near the river. Brenda quickly accepts the invitation and is ready shortly. She kind of likes spur of the moment things; she and Bill often just get up and go when the spirit moves them. It'll be a nice drive for a Friday night.

It's been about six months since the 'James' ordeal and of course every time Bill goes to the mountains he thinks of it. He had been asked by the authorities to report any contact with James if it ever happens. 'Sure, right away!' he thinks cynically. Even though he's been warned that failure to report contact means he's an accomplice ('and an accomplice to what?' he thinks) he will never reveal anything about his buddy. Time to get his mind back on Brenda.

'What a night to drive up to the mountains eh?'

'It's so beautiful this evening, I can't wait to get there' responds Brenda.

'Want to stop at the "Watering Hole" for dinner?'

'Yeah that sounds great, I'm starved!'

So the two stop for dinner at a favorite bar and restaurant on the way up and after a nice rack of ribs and coleslaw with some huge wedge French fries they're on their way again. Soon they arrive at the cabins and check in at the ranger station to get the key. Bill had called earlier and made the arrangements. It's very quiet and peaceful here. The other renters are not making much noise, and there are only four other cabins. They unload some gear and settle in to the small cabin; one bedroom a bathroom a small living room and a tiny kitchen is it. There are enough pots and pans to cook on the old wood-burning stove and there's an old well-used mattress on the bed to put your sleeping bag on. The living room has a rustic table and chairs and an old worn couch. There is electricity for lights and whatever electronic gear you bring. Bill fills the tiny refrigerator with the cooler items: beer, sodas, juice and milk and all the food for the weekend meals.

Brenda goes about tidying the place up and getting the bed made up with the two-person sleeping bag and pillows. She hangs up the clothes they brought and puts a few things in the old dresser. After these minor chores the two get a couple of glasses with some cream sherry and go outside. They toast to the beauty of the mountains and the evening, and before retiring sit out under the stars in a couple of old rocking chairs on the narrow wood plank you might call the 'porch'. The night passes.

There's a sunbeam coming through the window and right on Brenda's face that slowly gets her attention this Saturday morning. They both have 'slept in' a little, but not too much because the anticipation of the day arouses them.

'Come on sleepy head, make me some breakfast!' she says to Bill.

He just groans and rolls over.

'Come on, make me breakfast…'

'All right, all right… let me wake up will ya…'

Bill gets up and gets ready for the day then begins a great breakfast of pancakes, eggs and sausage. The coffee is on and a little orange juice poured and the table is set.

'Breakfast is so good up here! Is it the air or what?' asks Bill.

'Yeah, I know, I love it too. Everything smells and tastes so good.'

'What do you want to do today? How about a little hike over the peak and back?' asks Bill.

'Sure, that sounds good.'

After breakfast and cleanup and hanging around for a while, they get on their hiking gear and head out. As they're leaving,

Bill notices a guy picking up the garbage at another cabin. 'Maybe he's a janitor of some kind for the park rangers' he thinks 'a little scruffy though with the beard and all…'

The day is perfect; sunny and warm with a light breeze and blue sky with white puffy clouds dispersed all around. The hike turns out to be a lot of fun but very tiring and takes up most of the day. When they return, it's close to dinnertime. Bill gathers some sticks and firewood for the stone grill just outside the cabin. Steaks tonight! After getting the fire going, he turns to go into the cabin to get the meat when his eyes meet those of the man he saw earlier collecting garbage. The man is down by the farthest cabin looking at Bill with a smile. For a second Bill feels as if he knows this man, but his look he doesn't recognize. Then the man walks off towards the ranger station.

Soon the steaks are sizzling on the grill and Brenda is sipping her wine in the cabin while Bill chugs down a beer anticipating their cook out dinner in the mountains.

'Hey, how you guys doing?' asks a ranger walking past 'smells great!'

'We're fine, nothing like cooking out up here. Stick around and I'll put another steak on.' says Bill.

'Thanks, but I've got dinner waiting at the station. Sure looks good though!'

'I was wondering' says Bill 'I've seen this bearded guy around doing things, he work for you guys?'

'Oh yeah, that's old Wes. His name's Wesley James.'

'Is he a ranger too?'

'No, just a drifter we gave a job to about a year and a half ago. Think he's from North or South Dakota, uneducated. He used to do cleanup around here every weekend for a year, then we kept him full time. Doesn't make enough money to pay taxes, we pay him a few bucks a week from our miscellaneous fund.'

'So he lives up here?'

'Yeah, we let him use an old abandoned ranger observation cabin out in the woods for his home. Doesn't need much, and if he does we usually pick it up for him in town. Real nice guy and he keeps to himself, dependable too and always does his chores. Nothing to worry about, he stays out of the way.'

'Oh I wasn't worried, just curious.'

'Better get to those steaks, don't want to burn them!'

'O.k., nice talking with you, see you later…'

'See ya…'

Brenda comes out with some potato salad and sets it on the table they brought outside.

'Almost ready?'

'They're ready right now' says Bill 'get me the plates.'

Bill puts a steak on each plate and the two sit down to dinner. They don't talk much because they're both famished from the day hiking and they dig right in. After finishing as they're sitting relaxing at the table, Bill's mind wanders to the man with the beard. He knew that gleam in his eye when their eyes met but couldn't let himself accept the idea that it was James. After the ranger's explanation of the man, it began to fit together nicely, now he knew! Now it's Wesley, Wesley James. And he will remain Wesley James alone up here in the mountains, and Bill won't even try to get back with him much less tell anyone, even Brenda. He knows James is counting on his silence and trusts him as his best friend, his old best friend that is because now James can't be here, ever. Maybe Wesley will meet someone up here some day and have a wife, a mountain momma after all! He's already a friend with the rangers who bought his story and have no reason to talk to anyone about him. And even if they do, it's a good believable story.

It was a great weekend for Brenda and Bill and the drive back is very relaxing also. They both replay the good time in their minds and talk of the next trip they may want to take. Bill's mind takes another turn; he and Brenda have been partners awhile and really travel well together. They enjoy each other's company immensely, have a good spark of passion too, and they know of the mutual love they harbor inside for each other. Bill starts to wonder out loud:

'Isn't it true that one of the things that keep married couples together is that they're best friends?'

'Yeah, I think I read that somewhere…'

'Well, it only makes sense doesn't it? You can have the "hots" for a lot of people, people "in love" routinely break up! You have to have love but really be best friends, you know?'

'Married couples?' says Brenda.

ABOUT THE AUTHOR

Stanley B. Joye continues his writing with his second book containing two short stories for quick and easy reading. His life experiences and education, information derived from communication with individuals from all walks of life, and even public television is interwoven in his writing.

He delves again into one of his favorite topics, historical fiction for his first story. But this time in his second story he takes on a current topic of debate. He uses his own slant as well as other opinions picked up from the news and periodicals and creates a believable but somewhat peculiar story to bring forth some of these points.